St. John Chrysostom
Old Testament Homilies

St. John Chrysostom

Old Testament Homilies

Volume Three

Homilies on the Obscurity of the Old Testament

Homilies on the Psalms

Translated with
an Introduction
by
Robert Charles Hill

HOLY CROSS ORTHODOX PRESS
Brookline, Massachusetts

On the cover: Michelangelo Buonarroti, *The Erythrean Sibyl* (detail), Fresco, 1509, Cappella Sistina, VC.

LIBRARY OF CONGRESS CATALOGING–IN–PUBLICATION DATA

John Chrysostom, Saint, d. 407.
   [Homilies. English. Selections]
   St. John Chrysostom Old Testament Homilies /
   translated with an introduction by Robert Charles Hill.
      p. cm.
Includes bibliographical references and indexes.
   ISBN 1-885652-65-8 (v. 1 : alk. paper) — ISBN 1-885652-66-6
(v. 2 : alk. paper) — ISBN 1-885652-67-4 (v. 3 : alk. paper)
   1. Bible. O.T. — Sermons. 2. Sermons, Greek—Translations
into English. I. Hill, Robert C. (Robert Charles), 1931- . II. Title.
   BR65.C43E5 2003
   252'.014—dc22
                         2003003988

Contents

INTRODUCTION

From the beginning, in imitation of the practice of Jesus, Christian readers studied and meditated on the Scriptures composed by Old Testament authors. For predictable reasons, admittedly, they found them less appealing and more remote than the New Testament, if only because they read them in translation, just an odd exception being able to access them in the original language of composition. So they gave priority to the reflection on Christ penned in the wake of the Incarnation, and were prepared to capitalize on this priority in debate with those equipped only with Scriptures awaiting his coming. But the amount of exegetical commentary extant from patristic times on Old Testament texts, especially the Psalms, is but one index of early Christians' conviction of the divine inspiration of these works and the fact that their authors – προφῆται in the terminology of the creeds and the Fathers – were beneficiaries of enlightenment from the same Spirit as were evangelists and other ἀποστολικόι composers.

St. John Chrysostom shared this experience and this attitude with his predecessors, as emerges particularly in his commentary on many Old Testament works, as previous volumes in this series illustrate. He could access them only through his local form of the Septuagint (his frequent attempts to get beyond the LXX to the Hebrew original often coming to grief), and none of his commentaries on them measure up to his celebrated studies of the Gospels and his beloved Paul. He admits the priority he accords these New Testament works at the opening of his long commentary on Genesis:

> When Moses in the beginning took on the instruction of hu-
> mankind, he taught his listeners the elements, whereas Paul
> and John, taking over from Moses, could at that later stage
> transmit more developed notions.

On the other hand, like many of the Fathers, he is
concerned that his instinctive attitude should not encourage
his listeners to disparage this part of the inspired Word, which
after all was prescribed for reading and comment in the
synaxeis in which he acted as commentator. In his preaching
(on the Psalms, e.g., and during Lent on Genesis), he can
consequently be quoted for frequent endorsement of the
value of the Old Testament, its harmony with the New, and
the divine inspiration of the authors responsible for it.

> The New Testament and the Old come from the same Spirit,
> and the same Spirit who gave utterance in the New spoke
> also here.

> Do you see the relationship of both testaments? Do you see
> the harmony in their teaching? Do you see the consensus of
> Old Testament and New Testament statements?

The listeners of Chrysostom's homilies are left in no doubt
that the Old Testament authors on which he preached –
particularly the prophets and psalmists, προφητικοί all
therefore – enjoyed the inspiration of the divine Spirit.

Nevertheless, preacher and listeners both had to
acknowledge the fact that in their experience "the Old
Testament resembles riddles, there is much difficulty in it,
and its books are hard to grasp." Why should this be? There
is a paradox here: the authors are inspired by the Spirit but
not crystal-clear. Chrysostom, whose commentaries reveal
him having real difficulties in explicating obscure texts
rendered more obscure by a less than perfect Greek version,
devotes two whole homilies to accounting for the obscurity
of the Old Testament in general, which he sees as partly
inevitable, partly accidental. In this volume we see the

golden-mouthed preacher of Antioch facing up to this challenge, as well as commenting on several psalms (outside the larger collection of fifty-eight homilies already available in English) in which he sees the psalmist enjoying the inspiration of the Spirit. The translation of these six homilies completes the introduction of this score of Old Testament homilies by St. John Chrysostom to English-speaking readers in these volumes.

HOMILIES OF CHRYSOSTOM
ON THE OBSCURITY OF THE OLD TESTAMENT

Having long struggled himself with this problem of the ἀσάφεια of Old Testament texts on which he was called or chose to preach, and having (it seems) lately encountered an Isaianic text that, though "simple by nature, becomes difficult through the inexperience of the listeners" (not the preacher's, note), Chrysostom addressed himself to the issue in general. It seems he undertook the task at some point in his Antioch ministry, devoting part of one homily to it at a Sunday synaxis after a whole homily on the subject a day or so before, πρώ–ην; the homilies have thus become known under the rubric *De prophetiarum obscuritate*. His prompting comes from that Isaiah text together with the remark of the author of Hebrews, who on citing Gen 14 admits, "What I have to say to you is lengthy and difficult to interpret" (5.11). With such august encouragement, Chrysostom introduces his first homily with the admission we heard above:

> The Old Testament, in fact, resembles riddles (αἰνίγματα), there is much difficulty in it, and its books are hard to grasp, whereas the New is clearer and easier. Why is it, someone will ask, that they have this character, apart from the fact that the New talks about more important things, about the kingdom of heaven, resurrection of bodies and ineffable things that also surpass human understanding? So what is the reason why Old Testament works are obscure?

Doubtless his congregation appreciated his being so frank in sharing their bewilderment at the obscurity of authors who enjoyed the inspiration of the Spirit.

5

Chrysostom thus from the outset supplies the principal – and, in his view, essential and inevitable – reason for relative obscurity on the part of authors, albeit inspired and thus προφητικοί, who composed before the Incarnation. The New Testament is "clearer and easier" because it contains "more important things," even if these doctrines "also surpass human understanding." In the second homily, however, he will nuance this position somewhat by citing Paul's words in 2 Cor 3-4 about the veil that lay variously (in Paul's thinking, admittedly, as also in Chrysostom's) over the face of Moses and over the Law: the doctrines were present in the Old Testament, but were veiled. "Likewise the Law, too," he says, "since at that stage they were incapable of learning the perfect doctrines characterised by sound values (all these being stored in the Old Scripture, as in a treasure), had a veil, out of considerateness (συγκατάβασις) to them and to preserve all these riches for us, so that when Christ came and we turned to him the veil would be taken off." This nuancing brings Chrysostom's position on the Old Testament close to Augustine's dictum *in Vetere Novum latet, in Novo Vetus patet*, though bearing a typical hallmark of Chrysostom's thinking in the συγκατάβασις demonstrated for the Jews.

If Old Testament authors, then, though inspired, are essentially and inevitably obscure, there are accidental and circumstantial reasons as well. Firstly, there was fear of reprisals being taken against the Old Testament authors by the Jews if the truth was plainly told, and so it was deliberately obscured.

> In case the Jews should hear this clearly from the beginning and maltreat those saying so, they concealed the prophecies under the difficulty of interpretation and imparted to them great obscurity in the contents, ensuring by the obscurity of the reports the safety of the reporters.

Jeremiah's maltreatment at the hands of King Jehoiakim in punishment for plain statement of the impending catastrophe at the hands of the Babylonians due to infidelity is cited by Chrysostom as proof positive.

The further reason for obscurity, on which the second homily begins, is the matter of language: the Old Testament comes to us in translation. In rehearsing the need and process of translation of the Hebrew Bible, Chrysostom shows none of the uncritical acceptance of the legendary account of the origins of the Septuagint given in the Letter of Aristeas that we find in other Antiochenes, such as Theodoret; he simply states that such a rendering was necessary for the diaspora Jews "who had lost the Hebrew language."

> We do not have the Old Testament written for us in our native tongue: while it was composed in one language, we have it read in another language. That is to say, it was written originally in the Hebrew tongue, whereas we received it in the language of the Greeks; and whenever a language is rendered into another language, great difficulty ensues. Everyone versed in many languages is aware of this, how it is not possible to transfer the clarity naturally contained in the words when moving to another language.

So no matter how inspired the psalmists or prophets, they may be obscure when read or listened to in another language.

In preaching a further series known as *De diabolo tentatore* shortly afterwards, Chrysostom himself recalled the former homilies in reference not to Old Testament obscurity but to a moral codicil to the second one – "the day on which I discoursed on the need to avoid speaking ill of others." And it is true that he did lose interest in his chosen topic to take a customary digression onto the moral value of Scripture: "The reason we comment on Scripture is not only for you to get to know Scripture but for you also to correct your behavior" – a common theme of his, as of any preacher on the inspired Word. To us, however, these homilies delivered that week in Antioch, and now appearing in English, are of value in exploring the connection between the undisputed inspiration of Old Testament authors by the Spirit and the relative obscurity we find in them – a puzzle that occupied the Greek Fathers from the time of Origen, and puzzles modern readers as well.

Homily One

Proof of the obscurity of Old Testament references to Christ, the nations and the rejection of the Jews

Today I want to spread before you a banquet from the Old Testament, and the task I am preparing for is to direct my words to the ocean of Isaiah's wisdom. I hesitate and am afraid that on leaving harbor and approaching the depths of the inspired sentiments we may become dizzy, an experience had by less accustomed sea travelers. [1] I mean, when they leave the land and from both sides of the vessel they behold ocean and nothing other than sea and sky, they are overcome with dizziness and think the ship and themselves are surrounded by sea. The dizziness, however, comes not from the nature of the sea but from the inexperience of the mariners; other seamen, at any rate, dive into the waves naked without experiencing anything like that, descending instead right to the very bottom and staying there in greater safety than people living on dry land, and having no problem with getting the salty water in their mouth, eyes and whole body.

That is the kind of advantage that practice is, that is the kind of disadvantage inexperience is; the former in that fashion convinces us to scorn fearsome things, while the latter causes us to suspect and dread even safe things. People of the latter kind, in fact, even if placed on the top decks, get dizzy at the prospect, whereas the former are not alarmed even in the midst of the waves. This happens with our mind as well: waves of passion fiercer than those of the sea often lay hold of it, like a storm of anger turning the heart upside down, (165) and the winds of evil desire impart great confusion to the mind. The inexperienced and unskilled person, however, at the onset of the tempest of rage is immediately alarmed, disturbed, ruffled, and allows the soul to be submerged by the passions and suffer shipwreck, whereas experienced people practised in nobly bearing such things, like a steersman at the tiller, put their mind above the passions and do not stop adopting every means until they guide the vessel towards the tranquil harbor of sound values.

What occurs in the case of the sea, then, and happens with the mind is realised also in explanation of the Scriptures: there is need to be alarmed, disturbed when we go out on to the ocean, not because the ocean is fearsome, but because we are inexperienced mariners. It is possible, you see, that a text, simple by nature, becomes difficult through the inexperience of the listeners. [2] I shall cite to you Paul as witness: after saying Christ became a high priest in the order of Melchizedek, and inquiring who Melchizedek was, he went on, "What I have to say to you is lengthy and difficult to interpret." [3] O blessed Paul, what are you saying? Is it difficult for you with your spiritual wisdom, having heard words beyond description, being snatched up to the third heaven? If it is difficult for you, to whom is it comprehensible? It is difficult for me, he is saying, not from an innate difficulty, but from the limitations [4] of the listeners: after saying, "Difficult to interpret," he added, "Because you are hard of hearing." Do you see that it was not the nature of the text but the inexperience of the listeners that made difficult what was not difficult? Not only difficult, however: the same factor renders the short long – hence his saying it was not only difficult to interpret but also lengthy, attributing the cause of its lengthiness and difficulty to the hardness of hearing.

I mean, there is a resemblance to the situation of sick people: it is not proper in their case to provide an unvaried and hastily prepared meal, and instead one should prepare a range of foods so that the person tiring of one food may choose not to partake of it and may sample another one, and if they do not accept that, they may take another, and if they push that away, they may pick up something else. So we can overcome their likes and dislikes with the range of foods, and get the better of their being difficult to please with the variety of the meal. Often we have to do likewise in the case of spiritual diet as well: when we are infirm, there is need for a lengthy and varied sermon to be prepared, containing parables and examples, verbal tricks, long sentences and many other things of that kind so that from them all the choice of what is beneficial may be simple. [5] Even if, however, his treatment was "lengthy and difficult to interpret," he did not deprive them of the lesson of Melchizedek: by saying "lengthy and difficult to interpret" he aroused their interest so that they might be more interested listeners, and by providing the meal he pandered to their desire.

Let us also proceed this way: even if the ocean of the inspired authors is unlimited, and great depths are to be found there, (166) let us venture forth on the sea to the extent of our strength – or, rather, let us venture forth on the sea to the extent not of our strength but of the grace given us from on high, not with our confidence in mind but your welfare, imitating Paul in this, too. For proof, you see, that he did not deprive them of the treatment of Melchizedek, listen to what follows: after saying, "What I have to say to you is lengthy and difficult to interpret," he went on, "This Melchizedek, 'king of righteousness,' is then also king of Salem, which means 'king of peace,' without father, without mother, without family tree, having neither beginning of days nor end of life; resembling the Son of God he remains priest forever." [6] Did not Paul disturb your hearing in speaking about a human being and saying he was "without father, without mother"? Why say this about a human being? I mean, if he were to say this about Christ, would he not provide us also with a considerable problem? You see, if he is without father, how is he Son? if he is without father, how is he Only-begotten? After all, a son has to have a father; otherwise he would not be a son. But the Son of God is both without father and without mother. How so? He is without father in his generation here-below, without mother in his generation on high: he had no father on earth nor mother in heaven.

"Without family tree." Let those who pry into his being pay attention. Admittedly, there are those who take this term "without family tree" to refer to the generation on high. Some heretics in fact do not take this meaning, busying themselves about prying into it, while others, more moderate than they, concede the point, but they do not take the term "without family tree" to have further reference also to this generation here-below. Let us, then, bring out that Paul said this in reference to each generation, both the one on high and the one here-below: the one excites dread, the other is most mystical. Hence Isaiah also said, "Who will recount his generation?"[7] But, someone will object, he spoke of the generation on high. How, then, shall we reply to Paul, who spoke of both generations and then added "without family tree"? First he said, remember, "without father, without mother," and then added "without family tree" so that you might believe he is without family tree not only in respect of the generation in which he is without mother but also in respect of that in which he is without father – I mean the one here-below. Hence after citing both he then used the term "without family tree" lest, since even the one here-below is beyond comprehension, we presume even to snatch a glimpse of that other one: if the vestibule of the temple is fearsome and unapproachable, how will anyone venture to penetrate the innermost sanctuary? That is to say, while the fact that he was born of the Father I know, how so I do not know; while the fact that he was born of the virgin I understand, the manner even in this instance I do not grasp: the generation of each nature is a matter for confession,[8] and the manner of each is a matter for silence. As in this case of the virgin I do not know how he was born of the virgin but I confess he was born, yet I do not abolish the fact owing to my ignorance of the manner, so too should you also act in the case of the Father: even if you do not know how he was born, confess the truth "He was born." [9]

Even if the heretic says to you, How (167) was the Son born of the Father? bring his presumption down to earth and say to him, Come down from heaven and show how he was born of the virgin, and then put that further question to me. Hold him fast, keep at him and do not let him escape or run off into the labyrinth of his arguments; hold him fast, throttle him, not by hand but by word; give him no latitude for the distinctions and ruses he prefers. This is the cause of their instilling panic into those they debate with, because we follow their line of thought and do not submit them to the norms of the divine Scriptures. Let us, then, hem him around with a wall on all sides, the testimonies from the Scriptures, and he will have not even a word to utter. [10] Say to him, How was he born of the virgin? I am not going to budge or yield. He could not explain the manner, even if he were to try countless arguments. When God shuts the door, after all, who will open it? Such matters are accepted on faith alone. If, however, you do not go along with it, and instead have recourse to arguments, I shall say to you what Christ said to Nicodemus, "If I spoke to you of earthly things and you do not believe, how will you believe if I speak to you of heavenly things?" [11] I referred to the birth from the virgin, and you do not know or presume even to utter a word of it – yet you pry into heaven? Would that you were in heaven, then, and did not busy yourself with the Lord of heaven. "I spoke to you of heavenly things and you do not believe." He did not say, You are not convinced, but "you do not believe," showing us that even earthly things require faith. If, however, earthly things require faith, much more heavenly things. Admittedly, at that time he was talking to Nicodemus about a much less exalted birth:

the theme was to do with baptism and spiritual regeneration; but he said that even these things are comprehensible by faith. Now, he called them "earthly," not because they are earthly but because they are performed on earth, and by comparison with the generation on high which is beyond words and surpasses all understanding they are earthly. If, therefore, it is impossible to know how we are born again of water, and this happening must instead be accepted on faith alone, and its manner not pried into, what awful madness would be the cause of prompting human considerations in the case of the generation on high of the only-begotten Son and looking for an explanation of the manner of generation?

It has been sufficiently demonstrated, therefore, how the only-begotten Son of God is without father and without mother, and how he is without family tree in respect of each birth. Let us now return to the matter in hand, postponing the treatment of Melchizedek to another day, [12] and let us prompt your attention by the prospect of listening to the riddles of the Old Testament. The Old Testament, in fact, resembles riddles, there is much difficulty in it, and its books are hard to grasp, whereas the New is clearer and easier. [13] Why is it, someone will ask, that they have this character, apart from the fact that the New talks about more important things, about the kingdom of heaven, resurrection of bodies and ineffable things that also surpass human understanding? So what is the reason why Old Testament works are obscure? They forecast many troubles for Jews as well as the fact that whereas they will be rejected, (168) we will be given a place, and the fact that the Temple will be destroyed to rise no more, while Jerusalem will fall and be trampled on by all. Jews will become wanderers, and will be scattered throughout the world, driven from the city, no longer enjoying the ancient way of life, and instead all their former advantages wrested from them – inspired writings, sacrifices, priesthood, monarchy. And not only that: the Old Testament authors foretold many other such things, including countless tragedies in their own books.

So in case the Jews should hear this clearly from the beginning and maltreat those saying so, they concealed the prophecies under the difficulty of interpretation and imparted to them great obscurity in the contents, ensuring by the obscurity of the reports the safety of the reporters. Where does this emerge? An explanation is required of us, after all, even if we are among friends when we speak: perhaps there are also present many of those who are not friends. [14] So let them also learn this so that they in turn may become friends. I said that if the Jews heard the evils that were due to overwhelm them, and that on account of Christ Jerusalem would be taken captive in this undying captivity that is unchanging, [15] if they heard this from the inspired authors unmistakably, they would immediately have killed those telling them this. So where does this emerge? Firstly, from their behavior: they were frenzied and savage. The mob are always thirsting for the blood of the prophets, their hands were practised in slaughtering the saints. The mighty Elijah loudly levels this charge at them, "Lord, they killed your prophets, they threw down your altars." [16] Christ in turn, "Jerusalem, Jerusalem, you killed the prophets, you stone those sent to you." [17] Isaiah is in agreement with them in accusing them in this loud cry, "Your hands are stained with blood." [18] And Christ again, "Your fathers killed the prophets, and you build their tombs; go to the extremes of your fathers." [19] Do you see how the Master and the servants testify to their blood-thirst? What is the meaning of "Go to the extremes of your fathers"? Kill me as well, he is saying; add the slaughter of the master to the blood of the servants. In other words, if they slew countless people, though all fellow slaves, the extreme was reached when they laid hands on the Master – and logically so: as long as they did not kill the Master, they had hope of salvation, and had expectations that the lamb of God would come and take away the sin of the world; but when they slew the physician, violated the very mercy seat and turned away from the one who came to forgive sin, then they forfeited every hope.

Hence he says, "Go to the extremes of your fathers." Yes, he is saying, the fact that they are bloodstained and accursed is proved by many witnesses; but whence does it emerge that they would not have spared the prophets if they had heard that Jerusalem would be razed, (169) that the Law would come to an end, and the Old dispensation be changed? It emerges particularly from what has been said; but from the Scriptures themselves I shall proceed to make the proof clearer. You see, if ever they heard a prophet saying that Jerusalem would suffer an awful disaster, though they should have changed and averted God's wrath, they vented their anger on the prophet. For proof that this is true listen to the historical accounts. The Persians once besieged the city and a savage army camped outside it; the extent of the risk was quite obvious, the city of Jerusalem on the occasion being in the jaws of the trap. Yet despite the manifest nature of the calamity, when Jeremiah came and told them that the city would be given into the hands of the Chaldeans (though admittedly this was not prophecy: their eyes could see what would happen), he told them what was patent and before their own eyes; but those bloodthirsty people, lacking in perceptiveness and gratitude to their benefactors, were so crazed that they considered him a traitor and destroyer of the city, and said, "He is sapping this people's strength." [20] In fact he was strengthening them, in fact he was rousing their enthusiasm and leading them to God, building an impenetrable and impregnable wall around them; but those people understood nothing of this, and bade him be done away with: they always rewarded their benefactors with such recompense, and with the king's compliance they did not even stop at that, but when failing to do away with him they threw him into the mud-pit.

Now, if they did not give credence to a temporary captivity, how would they be likely to hearken to the prophecy of unending servitude? If Jeremiah had said, You will go off to Babylon, far from bringing themselves to listen to him, they would have punished him for saying it; if they had listened to the prophets saying, Not to Babylon but to every quarter of the world will you be scattered, never to return again, would they not have even drunk the blood of the speakers? If, however, this seems still to be guesswork, I shall provide you with clear proof that it was not safe for them to predict the future – namely, our dignity and their reprobation. Why was it, after all, tell me, that they stoned Stephen, the firstfruits of the martyrs? did they not level against him this charge, "This man speaks blasphemous words"? "He said," they went on, "'Jesus will destroy this Temple, and will change the customs Moses gave,'" [21] and for this they stoned him. Now, if at that time they could not bring themselves to heed this, even though the facts themselves at that time convinced them of it, how would they have put up with the prophets foretelling this? Having heard, dearly beloved, that they stoned him on account of the Temple and on account of the change in their way of life, hear how they leveled this charge against Christ as well. "This man claimed," they said, remember, "'Destroy this Temple, and in three days I shall raise it up.'" [22] Do you observe how in all cases the destruction of the Temple and (170) the change in their way of life instilled rage in them? For this reason, while the prophets made mention of it, they did not make obvious mention. Hence they wanted to do away with Paul, too, because he urged them to make a change in their way of life. Where does this emerge? "You perceive, brother, the countless numbers of Jews who have become believers, and they have all been instructed about you that you teach departure from the Law." [23] The faithful could not allow themselves to be taught departure from the Law: how could those who had not yet come to faith bear to hear that the Law at some time would come to an end?

So, on the one hand, the fact that the Jews would have killed the prophets if they had clearly foretold anything of the sort we have demonstrated from the testimonies – of blessed Jeremiah, Stephen the first martyr, Christ himself and the apostle Paul: finding the same charge against them all, they would thus have killed them. But on the other hand the fact that they would also have burnt the inspired books themselves if they understood their contents I shall try to establish from an historical account, hidden from you but about to become clear forthwith, as I shall try to bring it to you. For what the account is, then, listen. "It happened in the fourth year of Jehoiakim, son of Josiah, king of Judah, that the Lord said to Jeremiah, 'Write all the words that I have uttered to you from the time of Josiah to this day'" [24] – that is, all the evils I plan to bring on them. See what the loving and caring God says: since they could not bear to listen to any detail, he says, Sum all those things up and increase their fear so that they may reform by this means, at any rate. Remember the promise: the question is for us to show that they would have done violence even to the very books had they realised all the outcomes of this day. "'Perhaps they will heed the evils (the narrative must be adhered to) that I intend to inflict on them, and will turn back from their wicked way.'" [25] Does the Lord say "perhaps"? is he ignorant, tell me, of the future? is he unaware of whether they will heed, he who knows everything before it happens, who examines hearts and entrails, who discerns desires and thoughts, to whom everything is bare and laid open before his eyes? why did he say, "perhaps they will heed"?

It was necessary for you to learn this, too, you see, in view of those accusing the Only-begotten of ignorance. See, even the Father utters words of ignorance: the word "perhaps" is typical of an ignorant person – yet he is not ignorant. So when you hear something like this said by the Son, reach the same conclusion: as Son he imitates the Father in every case. But let the occasion for these controversies be put off lest we stray from the topic before us; let us instead ask why he says, "Perhaps they will heed." If he had said, "They will heed" without "perhaps," he would have been wrong: they were not going to heed. If he had told the truth, that they would not heed, it would have been pointless for him to send the prophet to people who would not heed. And it was not for that reason only but also to avoid his foreknowledge being thought a kind of coercion upon them to disobey that (171) he expressed it in a qualified manner, in case some should say that God had foreseen it, and it definitely had to happen. This is what they say about Judas, too: he foretold he was a traitor (they claim), and hence he became a traitor. What folly, what impudence! Foreknowledge, mortal that you are, is not in fact a cause of wickedness – far from it: it is not coercion for things to happen but only a forecast of them. It was not because Christ foretold it that the fellow turned traitor; it was because he was going to turn traitor that Christ foretold it.

Lest, then, in this case as well they claim that he said they would not heed and that he excluded them from the way to repentance, by anticipation he withdrew their pretext by saying to the prophet, "Perhaps they will heed." Remember the promise: I constantly remind you of this for this reason, that when I adduce the conclusion you may not forget what we were examining at the beginning of the question. [26] Now, what was it? That if the Jews had realised that the disasters that have befallen them were destined to happen to them (I refer to those that beset them today), they would have torn up the books and would not have spared even the divine writings. Let us come, however, to the narrative. On hearing this, Jeremiah summons his disciple Baruch son of Neriah, and says to him, Write in the book all the disasters that are going to happen to them. [27] What is going on? You get an order from God, and you send your disciple? you are not afraid, then? you are not troubled? you are not terrified? if you are terrified, how will your disciple manage? Nothing of the sort: the reason is supplied. After saying, "Write and read," note, he went on, "I am in prison, you see."²⁸ What nobility of spirit! Though he was in bondage, he did not desist from prophesying.

Let us pay attention to the righteous man's courage and the sound values of his mind. He did not say to him, Such awful disasters have happened to me on account of this forthrightness; I expended countless words, I gained nothing from it, nothing of any good came of it except my being terrified; God has not even released me from my bonds so far, and does he send me to the wild beasts as well? Nothing of the kind did he say or even think: he had in mind one thing, how the Lord's orders were to be obeyed; and since he could not manage it himself, he arranged for it through the disciple. Read it to them, he says, in fact, and tell them all the troubles; I am in prison, you see. Jeremiah dictated, and Baruch wrote it in the book. It was a period of fasting when this happened; a festival was approaching that summoned everyone to the mother city: it was necessary for a general assembly to be held since the gathering was due to discuss urgent matters. Baruch went into the rulers and read in their hearing all these words, citing also the reason, "Perhaps your plight will come before the Lord,"²⁹ in case they should think that he spoke as a prosecutor instead of realising he came to cure them, and so they would be more rational.

So how did they respond? Though they should have expressed their thanks, should have given commendations, should have marveled, they did nothing of the sort: (172) they went off and told the king the contents of the book, and took the book away to Elishama's quarters. The king sent Jehudi, the text says, one of his attendants, and bade him get hold of the book. The king was sitting in his winter palace; it was actually the ninth month, November in other words; he is numbering it ninth from Xanthicus – something we ought to be clear about. You see, if he numbered it from Dios, it would not have been the season for winter then. [30] Why, then, is this fact provided? You will see clearly from what follows. "There was a fire burning in front of him:" there were hot coals because it was cold. Do you see how nothing is passed over by the divine Scripture? A coal fire was in front of him, his lieutenants were standing around him; the book containing countless fine statements was brought in (prophecy of troubles, after all, is the end of troubles), and was read out. Remember the promise, I beg you. "As he read out three pages, he took his knife, cut them and threw them into the burning fire until all the book was consumed." [31]

Do you see how they do not spare even the books? how they cannot stand even the divine writings? Since it made mention of Jerusalem's captivity, he cut it in pieces; and unable to find the prophet, he vented his rage on the writings. The one who showed such hostility to lifeless things, then, what would he have not done had he found the living person? I mean, just as the worst of wild beasts seize those fighting them, at which these people take to their heels, leaving the skins in which they are clad in the beasts' mouths, whereupon they grind them up at the height of their anger, just so did the king, too. He did not find the owner of the book, and he cut the book to pieces – and not only cut it to pieces: he threw it into the burning fire so that not even a fragment of those writings would remain. You do not realise his frenzy, however; but you will grasp it clearly if you pay precise attention to the narrative: he did not say, Having read the whole book he burnt it – instead, "As he read out three or four pages, he cut them off." Instead of waiting to the end of the reading, he became exasperated right from the very beginning. For those reasons it was not safe for the prophets to read plainly to the Jews all the coming calamities: if he could not bear to hear of a temporary captivity, how could he endure learning of the continuing one? Nor did the king stop even at this: he sent men to look for the prophet everywhere, the text says, without finding him; God hid him, you see. [32] Whereas he hid this man in some place on that occasion, he hid the other prophets by the obscurity of what was said.

It is not only from these cases, however, that it will be clear to you that it would have been a reckless deed and the mark of a foolhardy soul to announce to the Jews the dignity and glory coming to the nations and the dishonor awaiting them: it emerges also from Paul's words. He at any rate saw a prophet giving a slight glimpse of this prediction and mentioning more clearly than the others both our (173) blessings and their troubles; he was struck and amazed at his audacity, and spoke this way, "Isaiah is bold enough to say, I have been found by those not seeking me, I appeared to those not asking for me. I said, Here I am, to the nation that did not call on my name." [33] To be sure, if there were no risk associated with the prediction, why did Paul say, "Isaiah is bold enough to say, I have been found by those not seeking me"? Actually, there was very severe condemnation of Jews: those not seeking him found him, and those seeking him missed out; those not hearing him came to faith, and those hearing him crucified him. Hence he called Isaiah audacious: he was really guilty of extreme audacity, standing in the midst of the accused, leveling accusations unmercifully, and openly excluding them from their privileged position by his prophecy while introducing to their glory those others. He had on the bench accusing him all those who had heard; and when jurors are hostile, who can escape risk? Hence his saying, "He is bold enough to say." [34]

I intend, however, to demonstrate this to you even more clearly. The reason that references in the Scriptures to Jews and ourselves are obscure is in case Jews should understand the statements ahead of time. As witness to this I adduce the most articulate Paul, speaking from on high, heaven's trumpet, chosen instrument, groomsman to Christ: "I promised you in marriage to one husband," he says, "to present you as a chaste virgin to Christ." [35] I adduce him as witness to you saying clearly that for this reason some things in the Old Testament are obscured, but not everything: if it was going to be totally obscure, there would be no point in things being said to the people of that time. After all, the inspired writings make mention of wars of the time, plagues and famines; they mention also things that are fulfilled today – the calling of the Church, the dismissal of the synagogue, the cancellation of the Law. These things, however, he did not want them to know – just the things happening in their own time. This is what I shall try to demonstrate, that he made only these things obscure – what had to do with us and the synagogue, present fulfilment, and the cancellation of the Law – which it was not necessary for them to know at the time. I mean, had they come to know from the beginning that the Law was temporary, they would have utterly scorned it; hence it alone he obscured. [36]

For proof, you see, that not all the Old Testament was obscure, and that only this part was veiled, listen to Paul clearly demonstrating to us both these things, that the Law was obscured, and that it was in this part alone: writing to the Corinthians, he speaks in some such fashion as this, "With hope such as this, then, let us employ great confidence, not like Moses placing a veil over his face lest the children of Israel gaze at the end of what was being cancelled. Their minds were hardened, however: to this day a veil continues to lie over their reading of the Old Testament and is not withdrawn, since in Christ it is laid aside." [37] Perhaps the saying is obscure; so we must render it clearer by recalling the story to your mind. When Moses had received the tablets on the mountain, remember, and was on the point of descending, (174) such an ineffable and marvelous glory beamed from his face that none of the general run of people could approach and converse with him.[38] So in case he be completely inaccessible to the people, a veil placed over his face made it possible for the Jews to associate with him without fear. While associating with the people he kept the veil on, whereas in turning to God he took it off again. Now, this happened for two reasons, both for making the lawgiver appear more credible to those who were due to accept the Law provided through him, and also for the purpose of having a type of the truth foreshadowed in him and the reason for the divine plan regarding Christ forecast ahead of time. Since, you see, some were bound to ask, Why did Christ not come with divinity revealed instead of being clad in flesh, the explanation was given to all these in advance through the face of the servant: if Jews could not bear to look upon the servant's glory that came to him later, how would they have managed to look upon the divinity clearly revealed afterwards?

That is not the only reason the veil is brought to our attention: it is because the Jews have the same experience of the Law as they then had in the case of the face of Moses. I mean, just as they did not see the glory of the face of the lawgiver since that covering was interposed, so neither is it possible to see the glory of the Law now. This is a point we have to make against heretics as well: they accepted this part of the letter in the belief that the words represent a condemnation of the Law; and hearing that the Law has a veil and that it is canceled, they took it to be an attack and abandoned the Scriptures only to fall foul of their own devices.[39] In fact, this very statement shows the Law to be really of considerable value: just as having the veil on his face was no condemnation of Moses at that time and instead was the Jews' shortcoming, it being actually to Moses' great credit that he had such marvelous glory in his face that a covering was required for the fellow slaves, so too did it turn out in the case of the Law. If the Law had not had unapproachable glory, you see, there would have been no need of a veil.

So when he says that "a veil continues to lie over their reading of the Old Testament," he is referring to its obscurity, whereas when he says that "it is not withdrawn since in Christ it is set aside," he indicated that part which is obscure. You see, that part of the Law was not obscure which was of help to us regarding our way of living; otherwise it would have been given to no purpose. Instead, those parts alone were obscured through which we succeeded in coming to know that it is set aside through Christ: this also is an effect of God's wisdom, his introducing the Law and saying of it that Christ would come and set it aside, and that in him it would come to an end. It is therefore only this particular part of the Law that says that in Christ the Law would be set aside that is obscure. The mighty Paul indicated as much in going on, "It is not withdrawn, since in Christ it is set aside;" in case on hearing that "a veil continues to lie over their reading of the Old Testament" (175) you might think it all unclear and obscured, he corrected the misunderstanding by the addition, saying first, "A veil continues to lie over their reading of the Old Testament," and adding, "It is not withdrawn, since in Christ it is set aside." This very thing is not unveiled, he is saying, that it is due to be set aside in Christ, and is not unveiled to those not making their approach in faith, [40] whereas the one making an approach in faith and enjoying the grace of the Holy Spirit no longer looks upon the Law with a covering over it, but perceives its glory unbared. It is the glory of the Law that it is able to teach the fact that it is set aside in Christ so that you may grasp this, too. Do you see the glory of the Law? Its true glory is when it succeeds in guiding you to Christ; [41] but it guides when it shows it is being set aside.

And so on this basis, too, the blow delivered to the heretics is timely: if the Law were contrary and inimical to Christ, and not given by him, Paul should not have nominated as its glory the possibility for its devotees to be taught the lesson that it is set aside by Christ. Again, if the Law were evil, its veil should not have been removed, and instead it could have continued to be obscured even after the age of grace. If, on the contrary, it is the role of grace to render its devotees more perceptive in grasping the Law with the result that they take from it every prompting and opportunity for faith in Christ, what could one mention as a greater sign than this of the kinship of the Law with grace, [42] that when Christ opens the eyes of those approaching him, they are able to discern the guidance of the Law, whereas when grace appears and becomes obvious, it succeeds with great ease in escorting those who understand the things of Christ? This shows that neither is Christ at odds with the Law nor the Law at war with Jesus – rather, quite the contrary: the one shows the way to this great value system, the other takes them from that point and leads them to the very summit.

For all this let us give thanks to the loving God, who has planned for each at the right time and has in divers ways been active in our salvation, and let us give evidence to the best of our ability of a way of life worthy of his lovingkindness and marvelous providence so that we may also attain to the good things to come. May it be the good fortune of us all to attain this, thanks to the grace and lovingkindness of our Lord Jesus Christ, through whom and with whom be glory, honor and power to the Father with the Holy Spirit, for ages of ages. Amen.

Homily Two

*More on the obscurity of the Old Testament,
on God's lovingkindness, and about not accusing one another*

A cowherd rejoices to see his herd of cattle prospering and healthy, and a farmer also rejoices to observe the crops ripening. But neither does a farmer so rejoice in his crops nor a cowherd in his cattle as I now rejoice and take pleasure in seeing this fine threshing-floor filled with these spiritual sheaves. I mean, when the preaching of religion is broadcast in the hearing of so many and such wonderful people, (176) of necessity the ear of response bursts forth in abundance and in season. [1] You see, when someone ploughs a rich and fertile field, even without sowing the seed with generous hand he will get an abundant crop, the nature of the ground of itself supplying for the paucity of the seed. Likewise, too, when you sow in souls that are convinced and brimming with piety, even though casting few seeds of instruction you will see a rich harvest, the wisdom of the listeners concealing the speaker's poverty.

It happens in fishing as well: even if the fishermen happen to be inexperienced and yet throw the nets into a bay that has many fish, they easily light upon their catch, the mass of teeming fish blotting out their inexperience. Now, if in the case of that catch the multitude of those due to be landed often makes up for the fisherman's lack of skill, much more will it occur in the case of this spiritual fishing: whereas those fish on seeing the nets thrown in leap out of the way and make off, you do the opposite. When you see him standing up to spread out the net of instruction, not only do you not leap out of the way and make off, but you even come running from all directions and move in further, each person pushing and shoving the next one in the effort to be first to get close and fall into the net. The result is that we have never drawn the net in empty, not on account of our skill but on account of your desire.

The other day also, therefore, the tongue flowing with gold tried and true regaled us sufficiently, containing as well streams of honey in its mouth – I mean the tongue of blessed Paul – or, rather, it blotted out even the enjoyment of any honeycomb with the sweetness of its spiritual teaching. Since by the values that become you, instead of even scorning me in my poverty and need, you admire on the one hand the words that are of a high standard and on the other you accept even our lowly words, I arise with enthusiasm to repay you the debt which I promised the other day but have not discharged, the length of the instruction preventing us from reaching the end. [2] What, then, was that debt? It is necessary, after all, to remind you of the loan so that the explanation may become clearer to you from the subject matter. We examined on that occasion, remember, why the Old Testament is more obscure than the New – perhaps you recall that – and to begin with we gave one reason, the brutish nature of the recipients, and we cited as witness Paul's words, "The same veil continues to lie over their reading of the Old Testament and is not withdrawn, since in Christ it is laid aside." [3] We showed that just as Moses the lawgiver had a veil, so too the Law had a veil, its obscurity; but the veil was no criticism of the lawgiver nor charge against the Law: it was due to the limitations of the recipients. [4] That is to say, Moses did not have a veil on his own account: it was because they could not bear the glory of his countenance; when he turned his gaze to the Lord, for instance, the veil was taken off. Likewise the Law, too, since at that stage it was incapable of learning the perfect doctrines characterised by sound values, both those about Christ and the New Testament (all these being stored in the Old Scripture, as in a treasure), [5] had a veil, (177) out of considerateness to them and to preserve all these riches for us, so that when Christ came and we turned to him the veil would be taken off.

You see, then, to how great a dignity the coming of Christ brought us, elevating us to the rank of Moses. But perhaps someone will say, Why was it told at that time if it was not due to be clear to them? So that it might be useful to those who came later: this is the value of inspired composition, [6] not when it announces present events, but when it forecasts future ones. Now, inspired composition, when it is uttered in shadowy fashion, becomes clearer after the outcome of the events, but not at all before the outcome. And so since at that time it was uttered in shadowy fashion, it was obscure; but when the events took place, consequently the utterances were clearer. For you to learn that inspired composition, even if uttered a long time beforehand and uttered in shadowy fashion, is more obscure pending the outcome of events, I shall give a demonstration from the disciples themselves. "'Destroy this Temple,'" Christ said to the Jews: when he chased those who were abusing the Temple with their trading, they said to him, "'What sign do you give us for doing this?'" In reply to this he said, "'Destroy this Temple, and in three days I shall raise it up.' Now, he was speaking about the temple of his body." [7] This is a kind of prophecy: the cross had not appeared at that stage, nor the destruction of the Temple, nor the resurrection after three days, for which he was responsible. See how he referred precisely to both, their effrontery and his own power; yet they still did not understand his words. While there is nothing remarkable in Jews not knowing, it says that his disciples did not understand, either, until he rose from the dead: "Then they believed the Scripture and the word Jesus had spoken." [8]

Do you see that they had need of the fulfilment in the events for the prophecy to become clearer, and that the Jews were guilty of nothing in not understanding those prophecies about Christ before the coming of Christ? In fact, it was by his coming that they were due to become obvious and clear. Listen to Christ himself saying, "If I had not come and spoken to them, they would have no sin." [9] Why would they have no sin if the prophecies had made a prediction? Because though they made a prediction, they were not clear or obvious before the coming of the one predicted. You see, if also at that time they had been clear and obvious to them, obviously they would have had sin even before his coming; but if they had no sin, it is very obvious that it was due to their obscurity and the shadowy fashion in which the utterances were made: they did not even require faith in Christ before the coming of Christ. So why was the prediction made at that time? So that when he did come they might have teachers of their own number to prompt them, and they might realise that what was happening was no novelty nor was the plan recently formed, and instead that this had been proclaimed ahead of time from on high even a long time before – a fact of no little significance for winning them over to faith.

This is one reason for the obscurity, then, which we demonstrated also with very many testimonies in the former discourse. Lest we irk you further by saying the same things, therefore, we must bring this to a close and mention a different reason, which is not obscure or unknown but which renders the Old Testament more difficult for us. It is one thing, you see, to be completely ignorant of the contents and see a veil imposed; (178) it is another to find what is said but to find it with effort. What, then, is the second reason why the Old Testament is more difficult than the New? [10] We do not have the Old Testament written for us in our native tongue: while it was composed in one language, we have it read in another language. [11] That it is to say, it was written originally in the Hebrew tongue, whereas we received it in the language of the Greeks; and whenever a language is rendered into another language, it involves great difficulty. All who are versed in many languages are aware of this, how it is not possible to transfer the clarity naturally contained in the words when moving to another language. [12] Three hundred years before the coming of Christ, remember, when Ptolemy was still king of the Egyptians, the Old Testament was translated into Greek for pressing reasons of usefulness and necessity. [13] You see, as long as it was addressed to one race of the Jews, it remained in the Hebrew tongue: nobody at that time was likely to be interested in it, the rest of the human race being reduced to utter savagery. But when Christ was due to appear and call the whole world to himself, not only through the apostles but also through the Old Testament authors (they too guide us to faith in the knowledge of Christ), [14] then it was that he caused the Old Testament works like some entrances and paths, previously closed by the obscurity of the language, to be opened up to all-comers through translation so that all who came flooding in all directions from the nations and traveling these paths might succeed through them in coming to the kingdom of the inspired authors and adoring the Only-begotten Son of God.

That was the reason that even before the time of the coming of Christ they were all translated, since if they had remained in the Hebrew idiom alone, and yet David had said, "Ask of me, and I shall give you nations for your inheritance and the ends of the earth as your possession," [15] how would the Syrian or the Galatian or the Macedonian or the Athenian have been likely to realise what was said with Scripture remaining in obscurity? Likewise, Isaiah cried aloud, "He was led like a sheep to the slaughter, a like a lamb mute before its shearer;" and again, "There will be a root of Jesse, and one rising to rule nations; in him nations will hope;" and again, "The earth will be filled with the knowledge of the Lord, like floods of water covering seas." [16] And David said further, "God ascended with a shout, the Lord with sound of a trumpet;" and again, "The Lord said to my lord, Sit on my right hand until I put your enemies under your feet." [17] Since, then, the Old Testament foretold the passion, the resurrection, the ascension, the seat at the right hand, his second coming and in short all the contents of the New (179), divine grace before the coming of Christ arranged for the translation of the Scriptures lest these things remain unknown to the nations due to come later and they be unacquainted with the force of Old Testament composition; it was to render them useful not for those from the nations alone but also for those from

Jews scattered everywhere throughout the world who had lost the Hebrew language.

Take, for example, the person from the nations who came to faith by looking at the Jews' signs. Likewise, how could the apostles have converted the Jewish person unless they had been in a position to produce an inspired author for them from their own number? If Paul on entering Athens, remember, made use of an inscription carved on an altar, and on that basis presented his teaching to them in the expectation of capturing them more easily by use of their own weapons, as actually happened, much more in speaking to Jews he required assistance from the inspired authors lest they in turn make the accusation that he brought to their ears some novel and strange ideas. [18]

Why, you might ask, was there not one language, and why were we not rid of the difficulty? [19] In olden times there was one language, my good fellow, and as there was one human nature, so there was also one language for everyone. In the beginning there were no people of different languages, there were no people of different tongues, there was no Indian, no Thracian, no Scythian: everyone spoke in the same tongue. So what was the cause of the problem? We proved unworthy of this one language, ever ungrateful to the benefactor. What do you mean, We proved unworthy of a language? do the brute beasts all have their own language – sheep baaing, goats bleating, a bull mooing, a horse neighing, a lion roaring, a wolf howling, a snake hissing – each of the brute beasts keeping its own form of utterance, whereas I alone am deprived of my own language? have animals savage and mild, tame and wild, continued from the beginning with their own individual language assigned them, while I their ruler enjoy less privilege? do their privileges remain intact while I have forfeited God's gifts? what awful sin have I committed? were not the former punishments sufficient? [20] He gave me paradise, and he drove me out of paradise; I lived a life

without hardship and free of effort, he condemned me to
sweat and hard labor; the soil gave me everything without
being sown or ploughed, he bade it yield thorns and thistles,
and he made me return to it again. He punished me with
death; he punished womankind with birth-pangs and labor.
Far from this being punishment enough, he also took
language from me, depriving me of this privilege so that we
might keep our distance from kith and kin like wild animals,
language acting as a barrier to my associating with them.

My reason for developing the objection was that on my
providing a solution the victory would be more conspicuous.
If his intention was to rob me of all these, you ask, why did
he give them to me in the first place? Do you want me to
provide the solution on this basis alone, on the basis of this
paltry objection? I mean, the justification on God's part is so
abundant that the objector's objection alone suffices to
dispose of the charges without any support from us. If his
intention was to rob me of all these, why did he give them to
me in the first place? (180)

In fact, I for my part ask the same question: if his intention
was to rob you of all these, why did he give them? And so,
since it was not his intention to rob you, hence he gave them
to you in the first place. What happened, then? God did not
rob you: you forfeited what was given. Be amazed at him for
his lovingkindness in bestowing the gift on you; blame
yourself for your indifference in not preserving the gift. [21] And
so it is clear that the one who gave it to you in trust is not
responsible: it is the one who betrayed the trust who falls
under accusation. He proved, after all, that he offered
friendship and lovingkindness and had the intention of
bestowing the gift, with no one obliging him or applying
pressure, with no works of yours to admire and no reward
for your labors to repay. Rather, as soon as he formed you, he
immediately conferred this privilege on you so as to indicate
that the gift was not payment of a reward but was a gratuity

and nothing else. If you did not preserve what was given, however, hold yourself responsible, not the giver of the gift.

Surely this is not all, then, that we can say of the Lord? While this defence is sufficient, to be sure, yet his unlimited goodness and ineffable lovingkindness supply us also with an abundance of further justification. It is possible, in fact, to say not only this, that it was he who gave it and you who lost it, the giver being innocent even in this of any blame – or, rather, deserving also of the greatest admiration for even knowing in advance that you would forfeit the gift and yet did not deprive you of it. Still, I can mention something else far greater even that this. What is that? That even after your losing it out of your own indifference, he gave back to you what was lost – or, rather, not only what was lost but even far more than that: while you lost paradise, he gave you heaven. [22] Do you see how much greater is the gain than the loss, how more substantial the wealth? He gave you heaven so as to give evidence of his characteristic lovingkindness and to vex the devil by showing that even if he devises countless schemes against the human race, it will be of no further benefit to him, God ever leading us upwards to greater dignity. You forfeited paradise, then, and God opened heaven to you; you were condemned to temporary labor, and honored with eternal life; he bade the earth bear thorns and thistles, and your soul produced for you fruit of the Spirit. Consider God's lovingkindness, I ask you, the extent he went to in making allowance. In the case of people who lose some of their possessions, even if they gain greater and more valuable things, they are anxious to look for what was lost and are not satisfied until they recover it. So when you lost paradise, he gave you not heaven only but both paradise and heaven: "Today you will be in paradise with me," [23] he says so as to comfort the soul of the grieving not only with the addition of the greater things but also with the recovery of what was lost.

If you do not mind, however, let us come to the matter in hand, and see how we lost language. The story, in fact, has no little bearing on security: [24] the person who gets to know the manner of the former security will be more careful in other respects. Now, it is necessary to mention everything to you – for example, that all people originally had one language, that it later changed into many; how long it was one, and when it changed into many; and whether that one disappeared and others came in, or that one remained when the others were introduced; (181) why they were confused and who was to blame; then in which of these many languages the Old Testament was composed (it was to do with it that we raised all these matters, remember), whether in the original and more ancient one or in those introduced later. But have no fear: even if we are unable to discharge the debt completely today, we shall discharge it all for you later. [25] Why, then, if we are not likely to discharge the debt completely today, should we read out to you the theme of the total obligation? So that in your expectation of the debt's discharge you may keep us constantly in mind. You see, the person who lends someone money and has them as a debtor imagines and dreams constantly about the one indebted to them – at table, at home, in public, in bed; and love of money ensures that that person and the money are kept constantly in the mind of the lender. So to ensure that we too would be constantly in your minds through the hope of repayment – at home, in public, wherever you are – accordingly though admitting the debt, we are not making the complete repayment today so that by the expectation of what is to come we may leave with you a reason to remember us.

Great, you see, is the security we have of constantly enjoying your love, being such a wonderful and numerous crowd; the person enjoying love, after all, will also have complete enjoyment of prayer. Now, the degree of good involved in this emerges from the following example. Paul, a man who was caught up to the third heaven, who heard ineffable words, who subjugated all the needs of nature, who was then in perfect security, needed also the prayer of the disciples, saying, "Pray for me that I may be delivered from the unbelievers," and again, "Pray for me that a word may be given to me when I open my mouth." [26] You see him everywhere both asking for the prayers of the disciples and thanking them after receiving them. I mean, in case someone says that it is through humility that he has recourse to the prayers of the disciples, he brings out their force as well when he speaks this way, "He rescued us from such awful deaths, and we hoped that he will also continue to rescue us, with you also assisting us by prayer for us so that thanks may be given on our behalf by many people for the gift given to us." [27]

If, however, the prayer of the multitude freed Paul from danger, how should we likewise not have high expectations of benefiting from this patronage? I mean, since we are weak when we pray by ourselves, but when we join together we become much stronger, we importune God by joining forces. Likewise, too, in the case of a king: in many cases after consigning someone to death and not responding to one person's appeal for the condemned, he is importuned by the petition of the whole city, and the man taken off to the dungeon he snatches from condemnation on account of the huge number of petitioners, and returns him to life. Such is the force of the intercession of the multitude. This is the reason we also all gather here, to win God over to mercy the more readily: since in praying by ourselves, as I said before, we are weak, bound together in love we importune God to give us what we ask. Now, I do not say this idly or for my own sake alone: it is for you to be ever prompt in attending the assemblies in case you should say, Why? can I not pray at home? While you can pray, prayer does not have the same force as when (182) it is done with its own members, as when the whole body of the Church with one accord sends up the petition with one voice, with priests present to offer up the prayers of the whole congregation. [28]

Do you want to learn how great the power of prayer made in church? At one time Peter was bound in prison, secured by numerous chains; "but ardent prayer was offered by the Church for him," [29] and immediately it freed him from prison. So what could be more powerful than the prayer which was of benefit to the pillars and towers of the Church? Paul and Peter were, in fact, the towers and pillars of the Church, and it loosed the bonds of one and opened the mouth of the other. For us to demonstrate its double force, not only from what happened at that time but also from things occurring each day, let us remind you of the very prayer offered by the body of the congregation. If, for example, someone or other should bid you pray privately for the welfare of the bishop, each person would find excuses in the burden being heavier for resting on their individual capacity; but if everyone together hears the deacon giving the direction in these words, "Let us pray for the bishop, for old age, for support, [30] that he may correctly discharge the teaching of truth, for those here present, and for people everywhere," you do not decline to carry out the direction; instead, you offer up the prayer with ardor in the knowledge of the power of your being together. The initiated are familiar with the words; this duty is not yet imposed on the catechumens' prayer for the reason that they have not yet advanced to this stage of public intercession, whereas you are bidden by the one leading the prayers to offer them for the world, for the Church spread to the ends of the earth, and for all the bishops governing it, and you respond [31] with enthusiasm, giving witness in action that the power of prayer offered in church with one accord by the congregation is mighty.

Let us return to the theme in hand, however, that in olden times there was one language. So where does it emerge that there was one language? "All the earth had one lip," [32]

Scripture says. The statement is obscure. Does the earth have lips? Not at all. So what does it mean, and to what does it refer? It is not referring to this earth, which does not have senses or movement: it was of the human race in general it was speaking, reminding them of their peculiar nature, bringing to mind the mother from whom they came. That is to say, this living thing is twofold – I mean the human being – composed of two substances, the material and the spiritual – I mean soul and body – having kinship both in heaven and on earth. In the spiritual substance, you see, it has fellowship with the powers above, and in the material it is related to the things of earth, being a close bond between both created things. So when it does something pleasing to God, it is called spiritual, taking its name not from the soul but from a different and higher status, from the action of the Spirit: the soul is not sufficient for us to perform good actions if we do not enjoy that assistance. For you to learn that the soul is not sufficient for us to do good actions (183) – why do I say, to do good actions? Not even to be able to understand the words, "Soul people are not in receipt of the things of the Spirit:" [33] as he calls those in thrall to the flesh fleshly, so he calls those leaving things up to human reasoning and not in receipt of the Spirit's action soul people. As I was saying, however, when we perform good actions, we are called spiritual, whereas when we sin and lose our way and do something unworthy of our nobility, it refers to us by our lowly nature, calling us earth. [34]

When at this place, too, then, it is on the point of accusing some of building the tower, carried away as they were into folly and getting ideas of themselves beyond their own position, and it is on the point of criticising their stupidity, for that reason it referred to their lowly nature in saying, "All the earth had one lip." For you to grasp that it gives us this name when we sin, it gave that name to Adam after the sin, saying, "Earth you are, and to earth you will return;" [35] in fact, he was not merely earth: he also had an immortal soul. Why, then, did he call him earth? Because he had sinned. At any rate, when he formed him, he did not give him that name. Instead, what? "Let us make the human being in our image and likeness; and let them rule the fish of the sea and the beasts of the earth. The fear and dread of them will be upon the whole earth." [36] Do you see how great were their natural privileges? how high the status? how remarkable the commendation? But that was before the sin; after the sin it was then "Earth you are, and to earth you will return." Listen also to Malachi hinting at this – or, rather, to God through the prophet: "See, I am sending you Elijah the Tishbite." So why is he sending him? "To turn the heart of a parent towards a child." [37] Since, you see, that fearsome and terrible tribunal was due to be erected, that prophet comes to refresh our memory lest the Judge take some who are without excuse and condemn them to liability to punishment, so that by his coming and prophesying that the coming is at the doors he might bring people to their senses, since what was said long ago normally falls into disrespect.

The fact that the sinners are called earth I must now demonstrate. After saying, then, "To turn the heart of a parent towards a child," he went on, "Lest I ever come and strike the earth harshly," that is, he will strike the sinners. Do you see the sinners called earth? Likewise when the prophet was discoursing on Christ, he spoke this way, "He will be girded around his loins with righteousness, and wrapped around his ribs with truth" [38] – not that rib and loins are applicable to God: he is explaining to us by this the incorruptible and infallible character of the Judge's verdict, and the fact that there will no longer be calumniators anywhere or spiteful people, nor will there be bribery or ignorance of what is right. In courts of that kind, you see, an innocent person is punished and a guilty one is let off: everywhere justice is corrupted; but when the righteous and infallible Judge arrives, the one whose loins are girt with righteousness and his ribs wrapped round with truth, everyone will get exactly what is just. (184) "He shall strike the earth with the word of his mouth." [39] For you to learn that he is referring not to the earth but to sinners, he went on, "And with breath through his lips he will do away with the impious." Do you observe that here, too, he called the sinners earth?

Aware of this, then, when you hear that "All the earth had one lip," take it to mean once again human nature: it reminds us of our own lowliness, there being great good in reflecting on our own kinship and knowing whence we have taken our being. This is sufficient instruction in humility, reflecting on nature: it can keep all passions in check, and bring peace of mind. Hence someone gives this advice, "Take heed to yourself:" [40] pondering your nature and make-up will suffice for you to keep yourself constantly in check. Hence that righteous man Abraham always had this thought on his mind, and never became self-important; though conversing with God, at any rate, enjoying such wonderful intimacy and receiving testimony from him to his virtue, he said, "I am earth and dust." [41] Another author, who means to keep in check the person who was puffed up, instead of going to great length simply reminds them of their nature and upbraids them severely in these words, "Why has earth and dust become arrogant?" [42] Are you telling me what becomes obvious after death? Keep people in check while they are alive. They are not aware for the present that they are earth and dust: they see the body's comeliness, they see influence, the flattery of sycophants, the suite of toadies. They are clad in rich clothing, they are invested with the heavy burden of office, appearances deceive them and make them forget their nature. We know that we are earth and dust, but we are the prudent ones; by contrast they do not look to the demonstration from their final end, nor betake themselves to the coffins and graves of their forebears, having eyes only for the present and imagining nothing of what is to come.

Teach them here and now that they are earth and dust. Wait a while, the author is saying, and I shall teach them not this but something else much more lowly so that whenever they get carried away, they may recognise their own lowliness, and so while still alive they may take the remedy. After saying, remember, "Why has earth and dust become arrogant?" he went on, "Because even in its lifetime its innermost parts are brought to nothing." What is the meaning of "Because even in its lifetime its innermost parts are brought to nothing"? The saying is obscure: [43] by "innermost parts" he means the entrails, he means the guts, the belly full of refuse and awful corruption and stench – not out of criticism of nature but for encouragement of humility. [44] "Because even in its lifetime it is brought to nothing." Do you acknowledge the lowliness and impermanence of our being? Do not wait for your last day to learn your limitations: study the human being while still alive, I ask you, descend in thought to its entrails, and you will see all its nothingness. But do not lose heart: God made us not out of hate but to spare us in this way by providing us with abundant occasions for humility. After all, if a human being, earth and dust though it is, presumed to say, "I shall ascend to heaven," [45] and had no natural restraint, to what excess would its mind not reach?

So when you see someone puffed up, (185) preening themselves, with haughty aspect, riding in a chariot, issuing threats, sending people to prison, despatching them to death, acting abusively, say to them, "Why has earth and dust become arrogant? Because even in its lifetime its innermost parts are brought to nothing." This can be applied not only to the ordinary citizen, but also to the one seated on the royal throne: look not at the purple, not at the diadem, not at the golden robes; study instead the nature, and you will see that it is has nothing more than the general run of people – or rather, if you prefer, run your eye over the purple and the diadem and the robes, and you will see once again earth as the common element in all of these. "All human glory is like a flower of grass,"[46] remember: see, all that finery emerges more lowly even than earth. Do you see how it keeps haughtiness in check? how the thought of nature itself demolishes all folly? It suffices merely to consider what we are and from what we were formed, and all foolish thoughts take to flight. This, you see, is the reason God formed us out of two substances, that whenever you get carried away, the lowliness of the flesh would keep you in check, and whenever you form an idea that is ignoble and unworthy of the dignity given you by God, nobility of soul may prompt you to emulation of the heavenly powers.

Now, acknowledgement of our nature is suited not only to the removal of folly; instead, even if some other desire proves an obstacle, even if this improper lust for money or for bodily things incites intemperance, this acknowledgement suffices to settle the passion. So whenever you see a shapely woman with shining eye, jocund appearance and cheeks resplendent, carrying some indefinable charm, setting your thoughts on fire and arousing your lust, consider that the object of admiration is earth, that the source of ardor is dust, and your soul will cease its struggle; draw a veil over her superficial appearance, and then you will see the actual lowliness of her shapely form; instead of stopping short at appearances, go inwards in your mind and you will find nothing but bones and nerves and veins.[47] But this is not sufficient? Consider what she is like, I ask you, when change has taken place, when she is old, infirm, eyes hollowed, cheeks sunken, all that bloom of hers disappearing: consider what you admire, and repent of your judgement. It is mire and dust you marvel at, dirt and ashes that sets you alight. I say this not to criticise nature – perish the thought; it is not to malign it or reduce it to lowliness, but to provide remedies for the ailing. The reason God made it like this, so lowly as it is, was to give evidence also of his characteristic power and his care for us, leading us on the one hand by the lowliness of nature towards humility and repressing lust completely, and on the other revealing his own wisdom in his ability to bring out such beauty even in mire.

So when I stress the lowliness of our being, then I unveil the artifice of the Creator: just as we admire sculptors to a greater degree, not when they show us the statue to be good for being made from gold, but when they produce a perfect and exact image from the clay of the original material, so too (186) we are struck by God the artificer and glorify him for imparting to our bodies a remarkable beauty and a demonstration of some ineffable wisdom in dust and mud. And he has done this not only in our body but also in the whole of creation: by bringing into being lowly substances on all sides, he has both implanted a clear sign of his characteristic artifice and embedded a kind of proof of the beings' limitations, for the purpose of your admiring the Creator for his skill and beauty, on the one hand, and on the other to prevent your worshiping what is made on account of the natural limitations and lowliness of the beings. The sun is bright when it shines, illuminating the whole earth; but when night comes, it fades. "What is more lightsome than the sun?" Scripture says, remember; "but even it fades," [48] not only at night but even in the day. The reason the sun often fades even in the day is, on the one hand, for you to admire the Creator for his artifice, and on the other to prevent your worshiping what is made on account of its limitations. Do you see this sky, how great its extent, how beautiful, how bright, surpassing our bodies in appearance? But it is lifeless. Do you see both the demonstration of artifice and the proof of limitation? do you see the aids available to you from both points of view? I mean, to prevent your criticising the Creator as limited, he made things beautiful, whereas to prevent your worshiping as gods what was made, he made them partly limited. Always be mindful of this.

The reason we comment on Scripture is not only for you to get to know Scripture but for you also to correct your behavior: if this does not occur, we are wasting our time in reading it out, we are wasting our time in explaining it.[49] You see, it is like a wrestler going into the ring, oiled and prepared by the massage of the trainer: if when the bout begins he does no justice to his training, he has wasted his time going into the ring. Similarly with your attendance here: if you learn all the devil's moves and holds, but at the time of the contest you stumble, through seeing a pretty face, developing a false sense of your own importance or being overpowered by some other evil thought, it is futile for you to enter here. Remember the words, then, not as being critical of our nature, but as being critical of intemperate desires; what is said is not an attack on nature: the statements are directed against lust. In this way repress anger, by these means tame lust, by these means bring self-importance down to earth.

"All the earth had one lip, and there was one language for everyone." See, the problem still faces us. The verse deals not with the earth but with the fact that all human beings had one language. But why did it refer to language by lip? Scripture customarily refers in this way to speech, language. Now, it is necessary to acknowledge this as well in view of the heretics, those who call into question God's creation, who claim that the body is evil. Since Scripture, remember, refers to the evil movements of the mind as the limbs of the body – to quote, for example, "They made their tongue as sharp as a snake's," "Their tongue a sharp sword"[50] – as a result some people think there is reference to the tongue. But there is no reference to the tongue – perish the thought: it is a work of God; instead, there is reference to lethal words that slay people, that assault them worse than a sword: (187) "Their tongue a sharp sword," and again, "His lips deceitful, he has spoken evil with a double heart," [51] referring not to a part of the body but to deceitful words. Using language in a similar way here as well, "All the earth had one lip," his message was not that all human beings had one lip: by "lip" he was referring to language; after saying, "All the earth had one lip," note, he went on, "And there was one language for everyone." Likewise when it says, "Their throat is an open tomb," [52] it is criticising not the throat but the evil words that come out of it, the lifeless doctrines: it is a tomb, a receptacle for lifeless bones and bodies.

Such are the mouths of those, too, who criticise the creator, such the mouths of the people whose utterances are vile, who voice abuse, discharging fetid and wicked words from their own throat. [53] Fill it with fragrance, mortal that you are, not with stench; make of it a royal treasure, not a satanic tomb. If it is a tomb, however, keep it closed in case the stench gets out. Do you have evil ideas? Do not express them in words; let them stay inside, and they will quickly be suffocated. We are human, we frequently form many plans that are wicked, out of place and shameful; but let us not allow the ideas to proceed to words, and so by being suppressed they may grow weaker and die. To make a comparison: if you were to cast different kinds of wild beasts into a pit and block the exit from the pit, you would easily suffocate them; but if you provided some narrow passage and airhole, you would give them considerable encouragement, and instead of leaving them die you would make them much wilder. Something similar happens in the case of evil thoughts, too: when they arise inside us, we quickly suppress them provided we shut off the means of their getting out; but if we bring them out in words, we make them even stronger by letting them recover their breath through our tongue, and we quickly descend to the depths of inappropriate actions from the attention to the shameful words. Hence the inspired author did not refer simply to a tomb but to "an open tomb," leveling the very charge I mentioned: those who utter shameful words shame not only themselves but also their neighbors, and bring great indignity upon their associates. And just as if we opened the tombs we would fill the cities with pestilence, so if we had no qualms about opening vile mouths we would fill all our associates with a worse disease. Hence the necessity of placing a door, a bar and a curb on our mouth.

The fact that at that time there was one language, then, I have sufficiently demonstrated to you; now it is necessary to explain why the numerous ones developed. For the time being, however, let us develop the more moral issue; let us teach the need to keep a curb on our tongue and not simply to give vent to everything that comes to mind, not to criticise the brethren, not to bite and devour one another. People who do this in word are worse than those biting the body: (188) the latter bite the body with their teeth, the former bite the soul with their words, they wound reputations, they leave an incurable injury. Hence the punishment and retribution they receive is the heavier the worse the bite they inflict. It is not on this account alone, however, that the critic does not attain pardon, but because he can cite no excuse, right or wrong, for venting his spleen: other sins, even if having an irrational basis, at least have a basis – for example, immorality fulfils desire, the thief puts an end to poverty, homicide brings anger to a stop, whereas the critic can claim no excuse. I mean, what kind of affluence, tell me, does he revel in? what desire does he fulfil? There is nothing other than envy as a motive, lacking any basis right or wrong. Hence he is bereft of any justification.

Do you insist on being abusive? I shall give you a useful motive. Do you insist on leveling abuse? Level abuse at your sins. "Tell your sins first," Scripture says, remember, "so as to be justified." [54] Do you see abuse rewarded with crown, commendation and righteousness? Again, "Righteous people are critics of themselves in their opening remarks" [55] – of themselves, not of another: if you turn critic of another, you are punished; if of yourself, you are crowned. For you to learn how fine a thing is criticism of one's own failings, "Righteous people are critics of themselves in their opening remarks," Scripture says. Actually, if you are righteous, how come you are a critic? if a critic, how come you are righteous? The righteous person is not guilty of criticism. For you to learn, however, that even if you are a sinner but criticise your sins, through your criticism you are made righteous, it therefore said, "Righteous people are critics of themselves in their opening remarks." Now, why did it say, "In their opening remarks"? Pay close attention. In court there are two groups, the plaintiffs and the defendants, the accusers and the accused, the guilty and the innocent. Here, on the contrary, the exact opposite applies: for your part as the guilty one, seize the initiative in your opening remarks so as to prove innocent; do not wait for the accuser. Even if you are among the innocent, still accuse your sins before you hear something of the kind from the other party. The tongue is a sharpened sword – not for inflicting wounds on others, however, but to lance our ulcers.

Do you want to learn that it was customary for the righteous to speak abusively not of others but of themselves? Listen to Paul crying aloud, "I am grateful to Christ for strengthening me, because he considered me faithful by entrusting me with ministry, though formerly a blasphemer, persecutor and man of violence." Do you see how he speaks abusively of himself? And again, "Christ came into the world to save sinners, of whom I am the foremost;" and again elsewhere, "I am not worthy to be called an apostle, since I persecuted the Church of God." [56] Do you see how he speaks abusively of himself in all places? He realised, you see, the value of this criticism in producing righteousness. So when there was need for him to criticise himself, (189) he employs the criticism unsparingly; but when he sees others also passing judgement on other people's vices, note the degree of severity he uses in silencing them, speaking this way, "And so do not judge before the time, before the Lord comes, who will bring to light the hidden things of darkness and disclose the intentions of the heart." [57] Leave the court proceedings to the one who knows the mind's unspoken thoughts: even if you are convinced that you know your neighbor's doings, your judgement is awry. "Who knows the thoughts of the human being," Scripture says, remember, "except the human being's spirit within?" [58] How many of the lowly and abject have the capacity to shine more brightly than the sun! how many of the high and mighty will be found to be dust and whitened sepulchre! [59]

Did you hear how Paul speaks abusively of himself, with severity and constant recollection of an exaggerated number of sins, for which he was not due to give an account? After all, though blasphemer, persecutor and man of violence before baptism, baptism removed those sins; yet he recalls them, not because he was due to render an account of them, but to demonstrate the lovingkindness of God, who made him what he was in transforming him from persecutor to apostle. Now, if a man like that recalls the sins that have been wiped clean, much more should we recall those committed after baptism: what defence will we have, what pardon, when he constantly remembers what was not held to his account, whereas we do not remind ourselves even of the sins for which we are due to give an account, and instead we pass over our own vices and busy ourselves with others'? [60] Listen to Peter saying, "Leave me, because I am a sinful man." [61] Listen to how Matthew, too, criticises his former life, calls himself a tax collector and is not ashamed to make public his former way of life. [62] You see, since they had nothing to accuse themselves of after baptism, they recalled their former sins, giving us a lesson in making no account of others' vices, on the one hand, and on the other in being assiduous also in constantly going over our own. There is not, in fact, there is not any other remedy so efficacious for wiping away sins as the constant recollection of them and the unremitting criticism of them. This is the way the tax collector succeeded in setting aside his countless vices so as to say, "Lord, be merciful to me, a sinner;" this is the way the pharisee forfeited all righteousness in neglecting to attribute his sins to himself and condemning the whole world in the words, "I am not like other people, rapacious, avaricious, nor like this tax collector." [63] Hence Paul also makes this exhortation, "Let each one test their own work, and then their boast will be their own work and not someone else's." [64]

Do you want to learn also the way righteous people in the Old Testament criticised themselves? Listen to how they, too, uttered remarks in accord with these people. David, remember, said, "My sins have risen over my head; they weigh me down like a heavy burden." [65] Isaiah cried aloud, "What a wretch I am, being human and having unclean lips." [66] And the three young men, confined to the furnace and surrendering their bodies to death for the sake of God, in their extreme situation listed their sins in the words, "We have sinned, we have done wrong" [67] – and yet what (190) was more illustrious than they, what more pure? I mean, even if they were guilty of some sins, that fire by its nature would have wiped them all out; yet instead of their eyes being on their virtuous actions, they reckoned up their sins. Daniel, too, despite the lions' den, despite the countless punishments he endured, criticises himself personally and makes no such remarks about his neighbor.

What, then? The person who speaks badly of others provokes the Lord, whereas those who speak badly of themselves placate and appease him; it renders the righteous more righteous, rescues sinners from their sins and makes them worthy of pardon. Aware of this, therefore, let us busy ourselves not with others' vices but with our own; let us examine our conscience, let us recall our whole life, let us pry into each of our sins, and let us not only not speak badly of others but also not listen to others speaking badly. There is, in fact, an awful accusation and retribution attached to this. "Do not give acceptance to an idle report," [68] Scripture says, remember: it did not say, Do not believe an idle report, but Do not accept it; shut your ears, block the entrance to the criticism, show that on hearing it you are no less an enemy and foe to the one speaking badly than is the one who is criticised. Imitate the inspired author who has this to say, "I kept after the one who secretly traduced their neighbor:" [69] he did not say, I did not believe, or I did not accept what was said, but I kept them at a distance like a foe and enemy.

There are some people, however, who comfort themselves with cold comfort by speaking this way: Lord, do not attribute this sin to me of rendering an account for listening. What value is there in the defence? what value in this excuse? Keep your mouth shut, and free yourself from charges; say nothing, and you are immune from the struggle. Why complicate matters for yourself both with God and with people? why make yourself liable to accusation? why saddle yourself with a heavier load? is it not sufficient for you to render an account of your own vices without encumbering yourself with other sins as well? This defence is futile: instead of being due to account for listening, you are called to account for criticism: when you listen, you do not keep your mouth closed, you are called to account not only for listening but also for criticising. Scripture says, remember, "By your words you will be justified, and by your words you will be condemned." [70] I make this protestation out of concern not for those who give ear to abuse but to those who give voice to it. The one who gives ear to abuse, after all, is not harmed or damaged; instead, if what is said about him is false, he even has a reward; and if true, even then he suffers no damage from the criticism: it is not on the basis of your vituperation that those making a judgement will arrive at a verdict on him, and if there is need even to say something extraordinary, the person bearing the defamation nobly will even gain a great advantage, as also likewise did the tax collector. The one giving voice to abuse, on the other hand, even if truthful in voicing abuse, suffers great disadvantage. While the fact that calumniators perish requires no proof, the fact that even if they speak the truth they make the tribunal more threatening by bruiting abroad the neighbor's misfortunes, becoming a cause of stumbling, revealing to everybody what should be kept secret, and broadcasting the neighbor's sins (191) is obvious to everyone. After all, if the person who makes an individual stumble will pay an ineluctable penalty,[71] what awful punishment will not that person endure who causes untold numbers to stumble through a wicked rumor? The pharisee, remember, far from telling a lie, spoke the truth in calling the tax collector a tax collector, and yet he paid the penalty.

Aware of this, then, dearly beloved, let us avoid criticising: no sin is worse or easier than this. Why? Because it is committed more rapidly than any other sin and quickly implicates the person not taking care. The other sins, you see, involve time, expense, premeditation and accomplices, and are often frustrated with the passage of time. For example: someone decides to commit murder, decides to rob, to take what belongs to another: much preparation is required, and in the process they often discharge their anger, lose their evil impulse, dissipate the corrupt attitude, do not translate the intention into effect. In the case of speaking abusively, by contrast, things are different: unless we are extremely vigilant, we shall easily be caught up in it; we need neither time nor preparation nor expense nor planning to speak abusively – decision alone suffices, and intention immediately takes effect. A tongue alone, you see, is called into service. Since the evil is swift, then, the sin quick to take effect, the punishment and retribution harsh, the benefit non-existent, neither slight nor great, let us take great care to avoid the contagion, and instead of bruiting abroad others' vices let us cloak them over. Let us exhort the sinners, as the Lord also says, "If one of the brethren sins against you, go, have it out between the two of you,"[72] and so the privacy of the charges will make the healing easier. (192) Let us not bite and chew others' wounds; let us not imitate flies, but emulate bees: flies settle on wounds, bees fly onto flowers. Hence it is the latter who form honeycombs, whereas the former carry diseases to the bodies they alight on; they are loathed, while the bees are desirable and welcome.

Let us, therefore, have our soul fly over the meadow of the virtue of holy people, and constantly stimulate the fragrance of their good deeds instead of biting the wounds of the neighbor. If, however, we should see some people doing the latter, let us silence them, stopping their mouths with the fear of punishment, reminding them of their kinship with their brethren. But if they do not respond to any of this, let us refer to them as flies in the hope that the reproach of this name may make them desist from their wicked occupation, so that they may rid themselves of this evil pursuit and devote all their time to studying their own vices. In this way, you see, the fallen will rise at the recollection of their sins that were not bruited abroad, those taking stock constantly of their own vices will easily set them aside, made more reluctant by the recollection of their sins to commit others, and those constantly observing the virtue of holy people will acquire great zeal for imitation of them. With the whole body of our church set to rights by these means, we shall be able with this full measure to enter the kingdom of heaven. May it be the good fortune of us all to attain this, thanks to the grace and lovingkindness of our Lord Jesus Christ, through whom and with whom be the glory to the Father with the Holy Spirit, now and forever, for ages of ages. Amen.

HOMILIES OF CHRYSOSTOM
ON THE PSALMS

For the early Church, as hopefully for the Church of our day, the Gospels and the Psalter were the spiritual classics *par excellence* that proved the staple for Christian commentators, congregations and readers. In a world of largely oral communication, believers were introduced to the evangelical sayings and doings of the Lord and to "the inspired composition of the mighty David" principally in homilies in church on the lips of preachers in a sequence of which we know little,[1] while other churchmen with responsibility for *cura pastoralis* – and perhaps without the flair of a Golden Mouth – committed their commentaries directly to writing.

The Psalms figured in the worship of eastern churches from the beginning.[2] Those included here, outside Chrysostom's larger collection and now appearing in English, show their purpose and liturgical origins being respected, the congregation singing one verse as a response to a text first read aloud and later made the subject of commentary by the homilist. Commentary on the Psalms was so far general practice in east and west that we have close on two score of works by the Fathers fully or partly extant from the third to the fifth centuries.[3] When Augustine, for instance, in 404 indicated to Jerome a willingness to compose such a commentary, his crusty mentor cited to him complete works by six Greek (omitting mention of Chrysostom – typically) and three Latin predecessors, plus other incomplete *in paucos psalmos opuscula,* to dissuade him from adding to the number on the grounds that if they were clear, his would be superfluous; if obscure, his would be presumptuous.[4] Thankfully, the bishop of Hippo was not deterred.

Antioch in its heyday saw a proliferation of commentaries on the Psalter. Augustine's contemporaries John (later to gain the sobriquet Chrysostom)[5] and Theodore ("the Interpreter"),[6] like their mentor Diodore of Tarsus,[7] both addressed themselves to the task before leaving the city to assume episcopal responsibilities in Constantinople and Mopsuestia, respectively; in fact, there is evidence that, perhaps honoring a predictable tradition, each launched his exegetical career with work on this classic.[8] Theodoret, bishop of Cyrus a generation later, somewhat under the influence of "the world's luminaries" as he terms these distinguished Antiochene predecessors, showed equal respect for that tradition by opening the preface to his Commentary in the 440s by admitting "it would have been a pleasure for me to do a commentary on the inspired composition of the mighty David prior to the other divine sayings;" but he succumbed to pressure to deal with other books first.[9] Thankfully, these Fathers' work on the Psalter looms large among extant remains in Greek, even if that of Diodore and Theodore is incomplete.

Chrysostom's works on the Psalms

Chrysostom, whose extant homilies on the Psalms are with this volume all now finally made available in English, in the course of his ministry both in Antioch and in Constantinople communicated to his congregations his own familiarity with the psalmist (David alone, in his view, as far as we can gather),[10] with whom he had an affinity as close as with his beloved Paul. What now stands as a collection of homilies on fifty-eight psalms was delivered, apparently in Antioch as a work of his early ministry there, to a congregation gathered not in a church for a eucharistic liturgy but in a classroom, διδασκαλεῖον, seemingly with men only present. We cannot be more precise; Photius, patriarch of Constantinople in the ninth century, admits, "We are not yet in a position to know anything about the historical circumstances of the commentaries, ἑρμηνεῖαι, on the Psalms except to marvel at the force and excellence in other respects of the language, and thus to say he completed them while at leisure rather then when involved in public affairs."[11] The latter judgement we may dispute, pointing rather to signs of youthful immaturity in composition.

Curiously, this major collection (we may not presume it represents a series) includes not all 150 canonical psalms, only blocks of Pss 4-13, 44-50, 109-118, 120-150. The fact is, however, that in addition to those homilies on fifty-eight psalms from Chrysostom's early Antioch ministry, we have several other particularly interesting homilies, some of which were delivered by him as bishop in church in Constantinople. These appear here for the first time in English. None purports to give a ἑρμηνεία on a whole psalm: two highlight the opening verses of a psalm that are used by the congregation as response, refrain, ὑπακοή – namely, 42.1-2 (a homily delivered in Antioch in 387) and 146.1-2 (probably Antioch); two dwell on a favorite theme, the evil and folly of riches, explored at length in a psalm's full treatment in the larger collection – namely, the single verse 49.16 (Constantinople, 399 – though it, too, is used as a responsorium).[12]

In that Chrysostom in delivering these homilies – for unlike the large collection of ἑρμηνεῖαι these were indisputably delivered to congregations in churches in Antioch and Constantinople[13] – is speaking at synaxeis that are eucharistic in at least one case, non-eucharistic in others, they are particularly valuable for showing him as liturgical leader, as spiritual and moral guide, as scriptural interpreter, and as homilist.

Chrysostom as liturgical leader

In a manner that appeals to us today, Chrysostom envisages the members of his congregations living religious and spiritual lives also beyond the confines of the church buildings in which they assembled to hear him speak and celebrate the eucharist with him. In his homilies on other books of the Bible, he had spoken of his listeners returning home to ruminate at the dinner table on the days' homily or "take the sacred books in hand and earnestly absorb the benefit of their contents."[14] In these Psalm homilies, too, he thinks in terms of the domestic church where the life nourished in his synaxeis is further developed.

> Turn your dwelling into a church: where there is hymnody, prayer, a choir of inspired authors, and the singers' God-loving attitude, one would not be wrong to call this assembly a church.[15]

If on an occasion the preacher has failed to do justice to the whole text set for comment, he leaves it to at least the more studious members of his congregation to continue their study of it.

Yet, predictably, he sets a high priority on their regular attendance at his synaxeis in church; and, as in other of his homilies, he can berate them for irregular attendance or – in the manner of preachers ancient and modern – castigate those present for the irregularity of the absent, as he does as bishop in the first of the two homilies on Ps 49.16. The church he sees as the ideal venue even for private prayer; when in the homily on Ps 146 he lectures on "the art of prayer," a term he had used in his ἑρμηνεῖαι in Pss 4 and 7, he gives a questionable recipe for devotion of reciting the words over and over again until no distraction interferes with comprehension, only then the pray-er being free to leave. We are left to presume from internal evidence whether a particular synaxis at which each of these homilies was delivered was a eucharistic liturgy or a paraliturgy of the

Word. Of the two homilies on Ps 49.16 delivered in
Constantinople in the wake of the fall of the consul-eunuch
Eutropius in 399, only in the second does he seem to be
presiding as bishop at a eucharistic liturgy and by right of
office speaking second, his homily thus proving relatively
brief and possibly delivered to a different congregation from
the first on that psalm verse. The other homilies by reason of
their length suggest rather a paraliturgical function,
especially in the case of that on Ps 146 delivered on Holy
Saturday, when no eucharist would be celebrated before the
Easter observance.

We are also left to internal evidence for precision on the
composition of the congregation at these synaxeis at which
he spoke, whether presiding as bishop or not. He delivered
the homily on Ps 42 in Antioch late in 387,[16] at a time when
he was an ordained priest, and he itemises the categories of
people present, at least by implication.

> So if on leaving you were to set eyes on some beautiful woman
> of loose morals enticing you and inviting you to love of her,
> say to her, I cannot go with you, I have made a covenant with
> God in the presence of the brethren, the priests, the teachers.

Presumably he includes himself among the priests, and in
addition there are present also teachers, διδάσκαλοι—
(bishops? unpriested deacons?). To judge from mention of
the particular temptation awaiting an unwary worshiper on
departure (the temptress lurks on every hand, in
Chrysostom's view), can we presume males alone attended?
A similar implication of an exclusively male congregation is
given several times elsewhere in this homily, while in the
first homily on Ps 49.16 in Constantinople Bishop John
justifies his attack on the rich by saying they are not likely to
get his good advice from their wives, who are good only for
"talk of finery and gold." Yet in that same homily he speaks
of provision for women attending the church in which he
was preaching, probably the Great Church in the heart of

the imperial city, evidently equipped with upper galleries:[17] the extravagance of their attire was so much in defiance of Paul's strictures in 1 Timothy 2.9 as to be a cause of scandal.

> If a pagan enters and sees those women so decked out up-stairs, and down below Paul saying this, will he not comment, It is all show and make-believe?

It may have been on other occasions, however, that women attended.

There is no question that Chrysostom sees particular value in his congregations' participating in the employment of psalms in worship by singing (if not the whole psalm) a verse or so as a responsorium, ὑπακοή, and that this practice was traditional in the churches of both Antioch and Alexandria.[18] That is one reason why he selected for comment in the homilies in this volume individual verses from Pss 42, 49 and 146, though admittedly 49.16 principally provided him with a cue for belaboring the selfish rich. There is no suggestion that he was himself musically inclined; he is simply justifying a practice that is in force in his churches. As he says of Ps 42,

> For the reason why it is recited to music, pay attention. Perceiving that many people are quite indifferent, are ill-disposed to the knowledge of spiritual things and do not find satisfaction in undergoing the labor involved, God wanted to render the effort more attractive and down-play the sense of labor, and so he combined the inspired composition with music so that everyone would be encouraged by the rhythm of the melody and direct the sacred hymns to him with great enthusiasm. Nothing, in fact, nothing so uplifts the soul, gives it wings, liberates it from the earth, looses the shackles of the body, promotes its values and its scorn for everything of this world as harmonious music and a divine song rhythmically composed.

Beyond the established practice of the Church there is for him the simple conviction that "music hath charms," though for one who does not show any of modern scholars' interest in *Sitz im Leben* and literary genres he does acknowledge (on Ps 146 in this volume) also that the psalmist composed these poems as liturgical hymns for singing to musical accompaniment: "Of old David sang in psalms, as today we do along with David. He had a harp with lifeless strings; the Church has a harp strung with living strings. Our tongues are strings of the harp which, while giving voice to different sounds, produce a devotion that is harmonious: men and women, old and young, differ in age, but do not differ in respect of melody, the Spirit modulating each one's voice and producing the one note in every singer." Even in the διδασκαλεῖον in commentary on the fifty-eight psalms Chrysostom had allowed for some such participation, though when arriving at Ps 118, where it is v. 24 that "is the verse for ὑπήχησις," he speaks of its being sung "at the heavenly festival" (Easter) for the reason that "the Fathers prescribed the singing, ὑπηχεῖν, of that verse by the congregation." Was it not sung at other times?

While Chrysostom accepts and endorses the value of sung prayer, however, it is in keeping with his rather pragmatic approach to "the art of prayer" that his accent falls on singing with understanding. On that Ps 118, while accepting the Fathers' practice of singing v.24, he had remarked, "We, on the contrary, must address ourselves to the whole psalm" for the reason that in his experience (as he remarked about Ps 141) "those singing it daily and uttering the words by mouth do not enquire about the force of the ideas underlying the words." Likewise, Ps 44.12 was customarily sung, but offered challenges to the singers: "The verse seems to be extremely unclear," he observed, so "pay attention so that your singing, ψάλλειν, may be done with understanding." This Antiochene accent on cognition rather than on mystical rapture occurs also in the homilies in this volume. While on Ps 42 he recommends following David's example to sing, he notes also Paul's advice in Ephesians 5.19 to "sing song and hymns *in your hearts* to the Lord," which he takes to be advice to sing with understanding: "What does he mean by 'In your hearts'? With understanding, he is saying, lest while the mouth is uttering words, the mind is off on its own, wandering in all directions, whereas the soul should be listening to the tongue." But he is realist enough to admit, especially of the domestic church singing along unguided, that at times understanding may come later: "Even if you do not grasp the force of the words, for the time being teach your mouth itself to say the words: the tongue is sanctified even through the words when they are said with enthusiasm." But it is only a provisional licence, "for the time being:" the ideal singer of the psalms joins mind to voice.

Chrysostom as spiritual and moral guide

Although Chrysostom recognizes in the David of the Psalms a paradigm of close relationship with the Lord, his Antiochene formation confines the spiritual guidance he gives his congregations to a pedestrian level. He is not adopting the role of a spiritual guru.[19] Even though the responsoria of Pss 42 and 146 are sufficient to prompt the reader/singer to intimacy with the Lord to whom they are addressed, Antioch's reaction to that approach to spirituality associated with the name of Origen prevented the commentator taking that direction, the result being "an asceticism without mysticism," in the words of Louis Bouyer.[20] Hence the accent above on staying in church till one gets the brain to follow the words, hence the insistence on singing "with understanding." There are rules for "the art of prayer," it can be learned (as he says on Ps 146).

> Do not neglect prayer: it is then in particular that God will be reconciled with you when you on your own account appeal to him, when you present a mind purified, thoughts that are alert, when you do not make idle petitions, as many people do, their tongue saying the words while their soul wanders in every direction – through the house, the marketplace, the city streets.

Worshipers in Antioch and Constantinople were to keep their feet on the ground.

That, however, was the world in which Chrysostom's congregations in Antioch and Constantinople lived – the home, the marketplace, the streets. He knew that, and was himself a close observer of life beyond the church. But like many a preacher before and since, his spiritual guidance of these lay people living in the world is flawed by his being willing to settle for homiletic platitudes that belie his own realism and his rejection of dualism in regard to material creation. It may be his pique at those absent that induces him to lash out in a tirade against the rich on Ps 49.16 that underplays the value of the this-worldly environment of his congregation.

> Where do you now spend your time, mortal that you are? In the marketplace. Amassing what kind of things? Slime and mire. Why go to the trouble of amassing money that perishes, covetousness that proves tyrannical, influence that perishes, a surfeit of earthly cares, here today and gone tomorrow? Why pick the blooms and ignore the fruit? Why run after the shadow and not lay hold of the reality? Why chase what perishes and not seek what abides?

Later in that first homily on Ps 49 he does abandon rhetoric to draw the necessary distinction for his lay listeners: "I say this to find fault, not with riches, as I have stated countless times, but with those who use a good thing badly; money is fine for good deeds." Despite this disclaimer, one feels that more frequent – if not "countless" – nuancing of his strictures may have helped the preacher in the imperial city live longer and be of more help to his flock.

For there must have been, one presumes, many rich people in Constantinople, and rich women in particular (including the empress?), who were left smarting under the rabid satire of wealth in itself and wealth abused that is the subject of the two homilies on Ps 49.16, "Do not be afraid when a person becomes rich, and the glory of their house is magnified." In rhetoric that closely resembles the complete ἑρμηνεία of Ps 49 in the large collection, the preacher lampoons the extravagance of rich people's attire, equipment of their servants and horses, houses, furnishings and way of life generally.

> What reason is there for you to have a gilded savage as your servant? what value is there in it? what good for your soul? what help to your body? what sort of introduction to your house? Quite the contrary: absurd expense, an outlay reeking of stupidity, a basis for licentiousness, a schooling in vice, an occasion for crude and promiscuous living, ruination of the soul, a way leading to countless evils. Couches inlaid with silver, gold-spangled, footstools and basins made of the same material, loud laughter – how does that help you get your life in order? what improvement did that do to you, or your partner, or anyone else in the house?

If nothing else, this would have contributed to the absence of many people from his synaxeis, as he laments. Women in general would have felt uncomfortable, even if not directly addressed, when feminine extravagance came in for particular excoriation.[21] The first homily on Ps 49.16, delivered in the Great Church where provision was made for women's attendance at some synaxeis, when a pagan (Chrysostom insists) would be scandalized to see their finery, develops into a digression on the virtue of hospitality exemplified by Abraham and his admirable wife Sarah to the heavenly visitants described in Genesis 18; and the women of his time and city are compared most unfavorably to Sarah, their extravagance being blamed for the "floods of tears" of the dispossessed poor.

The corollary of the extravagance of the rich is the plight of the poor, and it is a theme into which the homilist weighs heavily. Like his contemporaries he has no economic solution to the problem of poverty in his society: he can only recommend handouts in the form of almsgiving, as he does at length to his wealthy listeners. Yet he would strike a chord with modern conservationists in speaking of sustainable and just development of resources, a principle which the greedy rich violate.

> Since this lavish outlay does not bring even this advantage (posthumous esteem), then, let us avoid, dearly beloved, let us avoid the ailment, and not become wilder than the brute beasts. Everything is held in common by them – earth, springs, pastures, mountains, glens – and none has more than another, whereas though you are a human being, the mildest of living things, you become worse than a wild beast and swallow up in a single house the resources of countless poor people many times over.[22]

Generally, however, poverty and its solution are a moral, not an economic, problem for him.

For all his often intemperate rhetoric, Chrysostom is not giving his moral guidance as an uninformed recluse. He seems to know well the plight of the poor and the excesses of the rich (even if both Antioch and Constantinople homilies at times employ identical phrasing). He can document his lament of the evils of attending the theatre. When he refutes the objection by the rich that he is their enemy, he refers to a wide spectrum of society.

> Surely it is not you I am attacking? It is your vices. Do you not consider me a benefactor? do you not find me caring? do you not take me for a protector ahead of all others? who else will speak to you of these things? will the magistrate? Nothing of the kind – only charges and prosecution. Your wife? only talk of finery and gold. Your son? only talk of inheritance, wills, bequests. Your servant? only talk of service, slavery, freedom. Toadies? only talk of parties, feasts, meals. People at the theatre? only vile jokes and talk of unfettered lust. People in court? only talk of contracts, inheritance, freedom, crimes committed. Where are you able to hear about these things if not from me?[23]

He takes advantage of current developments in the imperial city to ram home his point, eminently, in the two homilies on Ps 49.16 delivered in the wake of the notorious fall of the

influential consul-eunuch Eutropius in 399, who could serve
as a glaring example of the dangers of life at the top.

Chrysostom as scriptural interpreter

It would seem, we noted, that Chrysostom had already cut
his exegetical teeth by the time he came to preach on these
psalms, the long collection of ἑρμηνεῖαι on the Psalter being
possibly his first work of biblical commentary (if we may not
speak appropriately of "exegesis" in these works).[24] His sixty-
seven homilies on Genesis are probably also to be assigned
to his Antioch ministry. As on those occasions, so in
commenting on these psalms he has open before him that
form of the Greek Bible, the Septuagint, that was in use in
Antioch, that we know from the Antiochene Fathers' use of
it, and that is referred to as Lucianic (on the basis of Jerome's
account of its origins)[25] or simply Antiochene. We need not
debate here its provenance[26] for the reason that in the case of
these psalms it reveals no distinguishing characteristics apart
from reading Ps 42.2 in the form, "My God, who is *strong* and
living," though he seems at that point to show knowledge
also of the more common LXX reading without the first
epithet. It may be because of the brevity of the biblical text in
these homilies which get no further than a verse or two that
Chrysostom is not tempted to dabble in the Hebrew original
of words, as he did with generally disastrous results in the
longer collection, and that he does not cite, as he did there,
the alternative versions we associate with the names of Aquila,
Symmachus and Theodotion, the only such reference being
in connection with Ps 63.1 in course of comment on Ps 42
(presumably through a copy of the Hexapla).[27] In short, the
nature of the task in these homilies does not involve the
homilist in textual criticism. His citation of the New Testament
in course of commentary on these psalms occasionally shows
characteristics of that similarly Antiochene form, which is
acknowledged in notes where it occurs.

Chrysostom proposes the psalm verses to his congregation not simply as the words of "blessed David" but with the even greater authority of the Spirit who inspired him to our advantage. "It was for this reason, in fact," he says on Ps 42, "that that blessed man sang the psalms for us – or, rather, the grace of the Spirit – not that we should merely recite the words, but that we should put it into action by our very deeds." All the (Old Testament) biblical authors are thus προφῆται and their work προφητεία. Furthermore, as he says on Ps 146 in an original notion to support his citation of the psalmist as a still living witness, the Scriptures are living images.

> After all, if a person sets up a lifeless image of son or dear one and thinks that person, though dead, is present, and through the lifeless image he imagines him, much more do we enjoy the communion of the saints through the divine Scriptures, having in them images not of their bodies but of their souls, the words spoken by them being images of their very souls.

The congregation, therefore, should listen to the psalm verse as a living text breathing a divine Spirit – a belief that invests it with great dignity and authority: "while the inspired author uttered it, it was the Paraclete who moved the author's tongue," he observes of Ps 146, thus launching into a statement of biblical inspiration by reference to that Ps 45 which so prompted the Fathers' thinking on the subject.[28]

For an Antiochene commentator in particular, however, that inspired character does not discharge one of the responsibility to take the human character of the text seriously, just as the human dimensions of the person of Jesus and of the process of salvation and spiritual development are to be taken seriously. According to his characteristic acceptance of divine considerateness, συγκατάβασις, manifested in the language of the text, Chrysostom insists on precision, ἀκρίβεια, in appreciating its detail.[29] "Each verse suffices to instil in us sound values, drill us in right teaching and be of the greatest benefit for living," he says of Ps 42; "if we examine each expression precisely, we shall reap great good." The corollary to this stance is respect for the divinity who speaks in human language and imagery; the divine beauty that prompted the psalmist to exclaim, "As the deer longs for running streams," should not be reduced to human dimensions. Anthropomorphic expressions require caution. While the psalm verses lose nothing at the hands of this sympathetic commentator, we might have expected him (were he back in his διδασκαλεῖον) to raise critical questions like the authorship of psalms and psalm titles as did his mentor Diodore; but in his pulpit that is not Chrysostom's concern. Nor would it trouble him if a modern critical scholar were to find that his treatment of Job at the opening of his first homily on Ps 49.6 did not respect the purpose of the author of that book as a whole (as is often true of preachers).[30]

Chrysostom as homilist

For full appreciation of these homilies, in fact, we should recall that they are the work of a preacher in his pulpit, preserved for us by the remarkable stenographic resources of the ancient world.[31] If the thought strays considerably from the nominated text, as it often does, that is what preachers do. If recourse is had to intemperate rhetoric, that is what impassioned preachers can be guilty of. If those present are chastised for the sins of the absent, preachers can do that, too. Chrysostom is preaching as bishop in Constantinople on Ps 49.16, an earlier speaker appearing before him on one occasion, and probably preaching as priest in Antioch on Pss 42 and 146. In all cases the day's text is read aloud, proclaimed, even sung by the congregation, and then preached upon: "Have you understood what has been read to you?" Chrysostom asks them at the opening of the first of the Constantinople homilies, and he begins the second with a comparison to sailors reaching port after the storm of Eutropius's fall: "Let us, too, imitate them, and rid of the uproar, disturbance and billows of recent days, put our soul in at the reading, ἀνάγνωσις, of the Scriptures as though into some peaceful harbor."

The homilist, well-prepared or not, speaking on a topic of his choosing or from the day's lectionary, could in the course of development stray from the psalm verse read out, even if he had previously treated of the psalm, as with Pss 49 and 146. Unless another speaker also appeared, lengthy development was expected, and the thread might be lost; the hospitality of Abraham and Sarah in Gen 18 takes over the first homily on Ps 49.16, as does the account from Acts 16 of Paul's delivery from prison in Philippi the homily on Ps 146, the mention of hymn-singing being the point at which the latter digression occurred.

If the congregation showed signs of impatience at the lengthy digressions, the homilist does not register them. They were at times complimented on their attention, especially at the beginning, as with the homily on Ps 42 and several in the long collection. At other times they must have been agape at the highly rhetorical denunciations of the extravagant rich or the vain woman, perhaps diverted to think of particular people they or he had in mind. At still other times their hair must have been on end as Chrysostom appealed to baser motives to stir them to action, as in the homily on Ps 42.

> If God wanted to bring to our notice all the favors he has bestowed on us each day, of which we are ignorant and un- aware, we would be unable even to number them. How many demons fly through this sky? How many hostile powers? If he only permitted them to show their fearsome and hideous appearance, would we not be out of our minds? would we not perish? would we not be destroyed?

Fire and brimstone have proved a stock-in-trade of preachers in all ages.

If long-winded at times, Chrysostom was, as his sobriquet confirms, never dull and never light-weight. Even if the topic for the day had expired, a digression was worth hearing, supplemented as it was with abundant scriptural documentation, particularly from other Psalms, Matthew's Gospel and Paul. His language, even when not highly rhetorical, was generally colorfully figurative, even if the figures were largely traditional; an original figure, like that of the Scriptures as living icons, was a rarity. The first homily on Ps 49.16 begins with such an appropriate – if hackneyed – image as to involve the audience from the outset: "While it is satisfying for a farmer to drive the plough to clear the pastures, dig the furrows, pull up the weeds and then sow the seed once no weeds are there to affect the sowing, it is much more satisfying to a speaker when he sows the divine thoughts among an audience that is free of disturbance." That final implicit reference to the fall of Eutropius would also serve to titillate the Constantinopolitan crowd.

There would be plenty to talk about on the way home from Chrysostom's homilies on the Psalms – or any part of the Bible. If a good teacher should bring together faith and life for his audience – and Chrysostom saw himself, even on a spiritual classic like the Psalter, primarily as a teacher – his later homilies on these psalms must be judged pastorally effective, even if differing in purpose and character from the fifty-eight *hermeneiai* in the long collection.

Homily on Psalm 42

As the deer longs for springs of water (v.1).
And why the psalm is brought into our life and recited to music.
And on God's longsuffering. [1]

The other day when we developed our treatment of Melchizedek [2] you were surprised at the length of our sermon, whereas I was surprised both at your enthusiastic attention and your understanding, and the fact that though the homily went on at great length, you paid attention to us to the end. Admittedly, it was not simply that the homily was lengthy, but that it also contained very difficult subject matter. So come now, let us repay that effort, and make our address to you today clearer; it is not always necessary to challenge the mind of the listeners, which is easily distracted, nor always let it go lax and slack – thence lies the way to easy habits. Hence there is need of a variety of forms of teaching, at one time applying more festive expressions, at another more contentious. So just I remarked on that occasion that when the wolves attack the flock, the shepherds drop the pipe and pick up the sling, so now that the feasts of the Jews have passed, who are the worst wolves of all,[3] let us in turn lay aside the sling and resume the pipe. Let us bring the more contentious words to an end and adopt some others that are clearer, taking David's very harp in hand and focusing on the responsorial verse which we all sang today.[4] So what is the response? *As the deer longs for springs of water, so my soul longs for you, O God.* (156)

Now, first of all it is especially necessary to explain why the psalm has been introduced into our life, and why this piece of inspired composition in particular is recited to music. So for the reason why it is recited to music, pay attention. Perceiving that many people are quite indifferent, are ill-disposed to the knowledge of spiritual things and do not find satisfaction in undergoing the labor involved, God wanted to render the effort more attractive and down-play the sense of labor, and so he combined the inspired composition with music so that everyone would be encouraged by the rhythm of the melody and direct the sacred hymns to him with great enthusiasm. Nothing, in fact, nothing so uplifts the soul, gives it wings, liberates it from the earth, looses the shackles of the body, promotes its values and its scorn for everything of this world as harmonious music and a divine song rhythmically composed. Our nature, at any rate, feels so satisfied and comfortable with songs and tunes that even infants at the breast crying and fussing are put to sleep in this way. Nurses, therefore, who carry them in their arms in their frequent goings and comings, soothe them by singing some childish songs to them, and thus close their eyes. [5] For this reason also wayfarers when driving their beasts at midday often do so by singing, encouraging them in the hardships of the journey by these songs. Not only wayfarers, however, but also farmers in the process of treading and picking the grapes, tending the vines and doing any other kind of work, often sing along. Seamen do it when rowing. Women at the loom, too, separating warp from woof, often sing a song individually, often (157) in harmony as a group. Now, they do this – women and wayfarers, farmers and seamen – in their anxiety to lighten the load of work with a song, as it is easier for the soul, if it hears a melody or a song, to put up with all the tedium and labor.

Since, then, our soul is naturally inclined to this form of enjoyment, God provided the psalms to prevent the demons introducing lascivious songs and upsetting everything, so that the upshot should be both enjoyment and benefit. From profane songs, you see, harm and damage and many dire consequences would be introduced; the more intemperate and lawless of these songs lodge in the parts of the soul, and render it weaker and more remiss. From the psalms, by contrast, being spiritual, there comes great benefit, great advantage and much sanctification, and the basis for every value would be provided, since the words purify the soul and the Holy Spirit quickly alights on the soul singing such things. In fact, for proof that those singing with understanding invoke the grace of the Spirit, listen to what Paul says, "Do not get drunk with wine, for that is debauchery; instead, be filled with the Spirit;" and he went on to mention also the manner of this filling, "singing songs and hymns in your heart to the Lord." [6] What does he mean by "In your hearts"? With understanding, he is saying, lest while the mouth is uttering words, the mind is off on its own wandering in all directions, whereas the soul should be listening to the tongue.

Just as swine make for where the mud is, and where there

are smells and aromas bees take up an abode, so where there are lascivious songs demons congregate, while where there are spiritual melodies the grace of the Spirit attends and sanctifies the mouth and the soul. I say this, not only for you to sing praise, but also for you to teach your children and wives to sing such songs,[7] not only at the loom but at their other occupations and especially at table. You see, since the devil generally lies in wait at parties with drunkenness, gluttony, ribald laughter and an undisciplined spirit as his allies, it is especially at that time that one ought, both before a meal and during it, ensure one's security with the psalms, and get up from table with one's wife and children to sing the sacred hymns to God. After all, if Paul, under threat of unbearable flogging, attached to the stocks and confined to prison, kept singing hymns to God with Silas in the middle of the night when sleep comes to everyone as particularly sweet, and did not succumb to the pressure of the place, the time, his worries, the tyranny of sleep, the suffering from those hardships or anything else to desist from singing,[8] much more should we in high spirits and enjoying God's good things direct to him hymns of thanksgiving so that even if something untoward happens to our soul from the drinking and the gluttony, all untoward and wicked ideas will depart once the hymn-singing takes over. And just as many rich people fill a sponge with balsam and thus wipe the table clean lest any stain of food (158) remain, and so present a clean table once it is removed, just so should we behave, filling our mouth with spiritual music in place of balsam in case some stain of gluttony remains on the soul, expunging it with that music and saying as we all stand, "You have given us joy, Lord, with your creation, and we shall rejoice in the works of your hands."[9]

Let prayer accompany the hymn-singing so that we may sanctify the house along with our soul: just as those who introduce actors, dancers and loose women into parties, thus inviting demons and the devil there, and fill their own houses with countless enemies (a source, therefore, of jealousy, adultery, fornication and countless other abuses), so those inviting David with his harp invite Christ to come in with him. Now, where Christ is, no demon would ever dare to gain entry – or, rather, even to peep in; rather, peace, love and every good thing will come in as though from a gushing spring. Those people turn their house into a theatre; turn your dwelling into a church: where there is hymnody, prayer, a choir of inspired authors, and the singers' God-loving attitude, one would not be wrong to call this assembly a church. [10] Even if you do not grasp the force of the words, for the time being teach your mouth itself to say the words: the tongue is sanctified even through the words when they are said with enthusiasm. [11] If we drill this habit into ourselves, we shall never by free will or indifference pass over this fine liturgy, custom obliging us even when unwilling to perform this fine worship every day.

In the case of this music, even if you are elderly, even if young, even if tone-deaf, even if lacking all rhythm, no blame attaches: what is required here is a vigilant soul, an alert mind, a contrite heart, robust thinking, a pure conscience. If you enter God's holy choir with these qualities, you will be able to stand next to David himself. No need of harp here, nor of taut strings, nor of plectrum and skill, nor of any instrument; instead, if you wish, make yourself into a harp by putting to death the limbs of the flesh and achieving great harmony between body and soul: whenever the flesh has no longings in opposition to the Spirit, but yields to his commands, and is finally led on a path that is sure and admirable, [12] you will thus produce a spiritual melody. There is no need here of a skill that is perfected over a long time; instead, there is required only a noble purpose, and in a flash we shall have the experience – no need of place, no need of time: in every place and at every time one can sing in one's mind. I mean, even if you go into the marketplace, even if you are traveling, even if you are in the company of friends, you can awaken your soul, you can silently cry aloud. That is the way Moses cried out, and God heard him. [13] Even if you are a workman seated in the workshop hard at work, you will be able to sing. Even if you are a soldier in attendance at court, you will be able to do the same thing. (159) You can sing even without a voice, the mind resounding within: it is not to people we sing but to God, who can hear even the heart and penetrate the mind's unspoken thoughts. In pointing this out Paul cries aloud, "The Spirit himself intercedes for us with voiceless groanings; and he who searches the heart knows what is the Spirit's intent, because he intercedes according to God's will." [14] Now, he said this, not because the Spirit groaned, but because spiritual men, those with the gifts of the Spirit, in praying for the neighbor and offering supplication did so with compunction and groaning.

Let us do so, too, and each day intercede with God in psalms and prayers. So as not only to offer up the words, however, but also understand the actual force of the sentiments – come now, let us focus on the very introduction to the psalm. What, then, is the introduction? *As the deer longs for the springs of water, so my soul longs for you, O God.* This is the way with lovers, not to keep their love a secret but to communicate it to the neighbor and say they are in love, love by nature being an ardent thing, and the soul not managing to conceal it in silence. Hence also Paul's statement of his love to the Corinthians, "Our mouth was opened to you Corinthians," [15] that is, I am unable to keep to myself and be silent on my love; instead, always and everywhere I carry you about in my mind and on my tongue. Likewise also this blessed man, loving God and on fire with love, cannot bear to keep silent, but at one time says, *As the deer longs for springs of water, so my soul longs for you, O God*, and at another, "O God my God, for you I watch at break of day, my soul thirsted for you like a trackless waste, waterless and desolate;"[16] as another of the translators likewise said; in other words, since he is incapable of demonstrating his love, he goes about searching for an example so as to convey his feelings to us, if only in that manner, and makes us sharers in the love. Let us take his word for it, then, and learn to love in similar fashion.

Let no one say to me, How can I love God whom I do not see? After all, we love many people we do not see, such as our friends in foreign parts, children and parents, kith and kin. No obstacle comes from not seeing them; rather, that very fact most of all inflames our love, it will increase the longing. Hence Paul says of Moses that he left treasures, wealth, the pomp of royalty and every other claim to fame in Egypt, and chose to suffer abuse along with the Jews; then, to give us the reason, that he did all this for God's sake, he went on, "He persevered as though he saw him who is invisible."[17] You do not see God, but you see created realities, you see his works, heaven and earth and sea. The one who loves, even if seeing the beloved's work, his sandal, his garment, anything else of his, is inflamed. You do not see God, but you see his servants, his friends – I mean, holy (160) men who enjoy his trust. Attend on them, and you will have no little easing of your desire; in the case of human beings we normally love not only our friends but also those loved by them. If one of those we love says, I love so-and-so, and if that person meets with good fortune, I regard myself as enjoying the good luck, we make every effort and trouble to give that person every attention as if it were our beloved in person we saw. It is possible to practise this also in the case of Christ here and now: he said, I love the poor, and if they receive good treatment, I make recompense as though personally enjoying it.[18] Let us do everything for their welfare – or, rather, let us divest ourselves of all our possessions to their benefit in the belief that it is God we are nourishing with these things. For proof, in fact, that it is he who is nourished when they are nourished, listen to what Christ says, "It was me you saw starving and you took care of, thirsty and you gave to drink, naked and you clothed;" [19] he gave us many opportunities to assuage our desire.

Now, the following three things in particular normally give rise to love in us: bodily charm, extensive beneficence, and being loved by the person; each of them in itself can prompt love in us. I mean, even if we receive nothing good from someone and yet hear that they continue to love us, praise and admire us, immediately we take to them and are fond of them as though a benefactor. In God's case, on the contrary, it is not these things alone, yet these three things can be seen to such an extraordinary degree as words cannot express. Firstly, the beauty of that blessed and unblemished nature, so extraordinary and irresistible as it is, surpassing all reason and defying all understanding. When you hear mention of beauty, however, form no impression of anything bodily, dearly beloved, but a glory that is incorporeal and a magnificence that is unutterable. To bring this out, then, the prophet said, "The seraphs were in attendance around him, and with two of their wings they covered their face, with two they covered their feet and with two they flew, crying out, Holy, holy, holy" [20] out of astonishment, out of admiration at that beauty, at that glory. David in turn perceived this same beauty, was struck with the glory of that blessed nature and said, "Gird your sword on your thigh, mighty one, in your charm and your beauty." [21] Hence also Moses longed often to see it, wounded by this love and in love with this glory. [22] Hence also Philip said, "Show us the Father, and it is enough for us." [23] No matter what we say, however, we shall not succeed in portraying even a slight or indistinct trace of that marvelous beauty.

Do you wish instead to list his benefactions? Yet even these language cannot portray. Hence Paul said, "Thanks be to the Lord for his indescribable gift," and again, "Eye has not seen, nor ear heard, (161) nor has it entered the human heart what God has prepared for those who love him," and again, "O the depths of the riches and wisdom and knowledge of God! how unsearchable his judgements and inscrutable his ways!"[24] Yet what words will portray the love he has shown us? Astonished by it, therefore, John exclaimed, "For God so loved the world as to give his only-begotten Son."[25] If, on the other hand, you prefer to hear his own words and learn of his longing, listen to what he says through the prophet, "Will a woman never forget to take pity on the fruit of her womb? Yet even if a woman should forget it, I shall not forget you."[26] And just as he said *As the deer longs for springs of water, so my soul longs for you, O God,*" so too Christ says, "As a bird gathers her chicks, I wanted to gather your children, and you refused," and again, "As a father has pity on his children, so the Lord had pity on those who fear him," and again, "Because as the heavens are high above the earth, the Lord extended his mercy to those who fear him."[27] As the prophet looks for an example to bring out his longing, so God also uses examples to make clear to us the love he has for our salvation. And as the prophet spoke of a thirsty deer and burnt up land, God spoke of birds' love for their chicks, fathers' care, height of heaven from earth and mothers' pity – not that he loves only as much as a mother does her child, but because with us there are no better examples of love than these limits, norms and examples. Since he does not love us only as much as an affectionate mother does her children, but much more, listen to what he says: "Even if a woman should forget her offspring, yet I shall not forget you." Now, he said this to bring out that his longing for us is more ardent than any affection. Taking all this into account, ponder within yourself, and you will produce an ardent love and light a bright flame.

Since among us human beings, then, nothing is so calculated to enkindle friendship as recalling kindnesses, let us do it in the case of God as well. Let us ponder all he has done for us, heaven itself, earth, sea, sky, the plants in the earth and the many kinds of flowers, cattle, reptiles, those in the sea and those in midair, the stars in the sky, the sun, the moon – in short, all visible things – the lightning, the good order of the universe, succession of day and night, the seasons of the year. He breathed a soul into us, he granted us reason, he honored us with supreme control. He dispatched messengers, he sent prophets, later his only-begotten Son. And after that he exhorts you in turn personally and through his only-begotten Son to be saved; and Paul does not cease acting as his ambassador, "As God is making his appeal through us, we entreat you on behalf of Christ, (162) be reconciled to God."[28] He did not stop even there: he took the first-fruits of our nature and "made him take his place above every principality, authority and power, and above every name that is named, not only in this age but also in the age to come."[29]

It is now high time to say, "Who will utter the mighty doings of the Lord, make known all his praise?" and that further saying, "What shall I repay to the Lord for all he has given to me?"[30] After all, what could equal this dignity other than when the first-fruits of our race, which has offended to such an extent and has been dishonored, is seated on such a height and enjoys such dignity? Reflect not only on the general benefactions but also your own particular ones, such as your being acquitted of accusation at a time when you fell foul of calumny, falling among brigands on some occasion at the fell hour of midnight and escaping their wiles, discharging a debt at some time imposed on you, gaining a cure when you contracted a deadly complaint. Reflect on all of God's favors done throughout your whole life, and you will find a very great number, not only in your whole life but even in one day; and if God wanted to bring to our notice all the favors he has bestowed on us each day, of which we are ignorant and unaware, we would be unable even to number them. How many demons fly through this sky? How many hostile powers? If he only permitted them to show their fearsome and hideous appearance, would we not be out of our minds? would we not perish? would we not be destroyed? [31]

Reflecting on all these, and all the sins we commit willingly or unknowingly (it being no slight matter for gratitude that each day God does not take action for our sins), we shall be in a position to love God. After all, when you consider all the sins you commit each day, all the favors he does each day, how much longsuffering you enjoy, how much forgiveness, and that if God took action each day, you would not live for the briefest period (according to the prophet's saying, "If you, Lord, were to observe iniquities, Lord, who would bear it?"), [32] you would give thanks to him and complain of none of the things that befall you. On the contrary, you would see that even if you suffered countless troubles, you would not yet have paid sufficient penalty, and with this disposition you would enkindle a lively desire and be able to say with the inspired author, *As the deer longs for the springs of waters, so my soul longs for you, O God.*

Now, it is worth examining why on earth he brought this animal to our attention. The deer is somehow a thirsty creature, and for this reason it constantly betakes itself to springs of water. Now, it is thirsty both by nature and by eating snakes and being nourished on their bodies. [33] Do likewise in your own case: eat the spiritual snake, dash sin to the ground and you will be in a position to thirst with a longing for God. You see, just as a bad conscience makes us dirty and drives us to despair, so (163) if we dash our sins to the ground, if we purge wickedness, we shall be in a position to look forward to the spiritual longing and with great enthusiasm call on God, enkindle love more ardently and sing this refrain not only in words but also in our very deeds. It was for this reason, in fact, that that blessed man sang the psalms for us – or, rather, the grace of the Spirit [34] – not that we should merely recite the words, but that we should put it into action by our very deeds. So do not have the idea of entering here for this reason, simply to recite the words, but so that when you sing the refrain, you regard the refrain as a covenant: when you said *As the deer longs for springs of water, so my soul longs for you, O God*, you made a covenant with God, you signed a deed without paper or ink, in words confessing that you love him above everything, that you prefer nothing to him, and are on fire with love for him. So if on leaving you were to set eyes on some beautiful woman of loose morals enticing you and inviting you to love of her, say to her, I cannot go with you, I have made a covenant with God in the presence of the brethren, the priests, the teachers, [35] I have made my profession of faith and promised to love him in the response that goes like this, *As the deer longs for springs of water*. I am in fear of breaking the covenant, from now on I am putting love for him into practice. If you espy money lying in the marketplace or garments of gold, other people swaggering about with servants and horses with golden bridles, do not be affected by that display, but sing to yourself once more and say to your soul, We were just now singing the refrain *As the deer longs for springs of water, so my soul longs for you, O God*, we claimed the text for ourselves and made it our own.

Let us love nothing of this life, therefore, so that that other love may remain unsullied and not be weakened by being divided. This wealth will be able to regale us with complete wealth, complete treasure, complete reputation, complete glory, complete fame. Let us hold it fast, and we shall have no need of anything else. After all, if those who go after that other kind of love, on fire with lust for some pretty girl, despite the threats of parents, the taunts of friends, and the criticism of many others are not put off, and instead are set on that girl and have only scorn for home, patrimony, glory, reputation and friends' advice in the belief that they have compensation for all this in the good opinion of the beloved alone, no matter how vile, how worthless and otherwise disreputable she be, will those who love God as they should ever be influenced by human considerations, be they fair or foul? In directing their love to him they will therefore not even have an eye for the mirages of the present life, instead mocking all its good fortune, on the one hand, and on the other despising misfortune, being held fast by the longing for God, seeing nothing else than him alone, keeping him everywhere in their mind's eye and regarding themselves more blessed than anyone. Be they in need, in dishonor, in bonds, in distress, in extreme trouble, they will consider they are better placed even than monarchs, in all their sufferings gaining a wonderful consolation from the fact that they suffer them for the sake of the one for whom they long. (164)

This was the reason why Paul, too, in dying daily, in confinement, in shipwreck, in scourging, in countless other punishments rejoiced and was glad, he exulted and was boastful. At one time he said, "We boast not only of the hope of the glory of God, but also in our tribulations," at another time, "I rejoice in the sufferings, and in my flesh I am completing what is lacking in Christ's afflictions," and he calls it a grace, confessing in these terms and saying, "We have thus been granted the privilege by Christ not only of believing in him but also of suffering for him." [36] Let us also have such an attitude, then, and we shall bear with pleasure all the misfortunes befalling us.

Now, we shall be able to bear them if we love God as the inspired author loved: you can see it not only in the refrain but also in the following words, where after saying *As the deer longs for springs of water, so my soul longed for you, my God*, he went on *My soul thirsted for God, who is strong and living: when shall I come and see the face of God?* (v.2). He did not say, My soul loved the living God, [37] or My soul was enamored of the living God; rather, to bring out his feelings he referred to love as *thirst*, indicating both things to us, the ardor of the love and the permanence of the desire. In other words, just as those who are thirsty do not have this feeling for a single day or several but for the whole of their life, their nature being the basis for it, so too that blessed man and all holy people did not feel compunction for one day only, as do many people, nor for several – nothing surprising in this; instead, constantly and day in day out they continue to love reverently, and they deepen the love. This, then, was what he also was stressing in saying *My soul thirsted for God, who is strong and living*, at the one time meaning to state the cause and wanting for your sake to bring out how a person would love God in this way. In what follows, in fact, he indicated this by saying *My soul thirsted for God* and added *who is living* as if exhorting and exclaiming to everyone hankering after the things of this life, Why are you mad about bodies? why do you desire reputation? why do you lust for the good life? None of these abides and lives forever: they ebb and flow and pass away, they are of no more substance than a shadow, more deceptive than dreams and more evanescent than spring flowers, some disappearing with the present life, others perishing even beforehand. Possession of them is unreliable, enjoyment insecure, change rapid. With God, on the contrary, there is nothing of the kind: he lives and abides without end, undergoing no change or transformation.

Bypassing what is temporary and passing, therefore, let us love the one who is everlasting and constant. After all, it is impossible for the one loving him ever to be confounded, impossible to suffer shipwreck, impossible to be bereft of the beloved. The one who loves money will be stripped of what he desires either with the onset of death or even before death, and the one in love with reputation (165) here and now suffers the same fate, and often even bodily beauty is snuffed out more quickly than the aforesaid, and in short all earthly things, being temporary and passing, promptly take their leave, even before they come to be and appear. The love of all spiritual things, on the contrary, ever blooms and flourishes, does not feel the passing of the years, undergoes no ageing, is not liable to any change or transformation or uncertainty about the future; instead, it is of advantage even to those with possessions here, protects them on all sides, does not leave them when they pass on, but accompanies them on the journey and helps them make the change, and on that day it renders them more splendid than the heavenly bodies themselves.

Aware of this, therefore, blessed David continued loving, and could not bear to hold his love in, but was anxious to show in every way to the listeners the fire that burned within him: after saying *My soul thirsted for God, who is strong and living*, he went on *When shall I come and see the face of God?* Observe the person on fire, observe him aflame. Knowing that on departing from this life he would see him, he does not abide any postponement or brook any delay; instead, in this case he reveals to us the attitude of the apostle, who groaned at the prospect of his impending departure from this life, [38] an experience our composer also had – hence his saying, *When shall I come and see the face of God?* If he had been some private citizen, of obscure origins, unimportant, living in poverty, it would still have been remarkable for him to scorn the present life in this way – but not so remarkable as in this case of a man on the throne, enjoying a life of such luxury, recipient of such attention, victor in so many contests, winner of so many wars, famous and acclaimed on all sides, and yet mocking all this – all wealth, glory, fine living – and hankering after future goods. This is the mark of a magnanimous mind, this the sign of a soul imbued with sound values and buoyed up with heavenly love.

Let us, too, imitate him and not admire this life so that we may admire the future – or, rather, let us admire the future so that we may not admire the present. After all, if we constantly put our mind to those things – the kingdom of heaven, immortality, life without end, joining the angels, life with Christ, that untarnished glory – and if we ponder within ourselves a life rid of all pain, and observe that weeping, taunts, abuse, death, depression, hardship, old age, disease, ill-health, poverty, calumny, widowhood, sin, condemnation, punishment, retribution and anything else in the present life that is bitter and unpleasant is completely banished, while their place is taken by peace, gentleness, simplicity, love, joy, glory, respect, fame and everything else that defies description, no present reality will captivate us, and instead we too shall be able to say with the inspired author, *When shall I come and see the face of God?* If we have this attitude, we shall not be attracted to folly by life's glitter, nor to depression by life's disappointments; no envy, no (166) vainglory, nothing of this kind will ever captivate us. [39]

Let us, therefore, not enter here idly, nor casually utter the refrains; instead, let us leave using them like a badge of office. Each verse suffices to instil in us sound values, drill us in right teaching and be of the greatest benefit for living; if we examine each expression precisely, [40] we shall reap great good. We should not, in fact, claim poverty, business or timidity as an excuse in this case: if you are poor and are short of books on account of poverty, or if you own books but have not the time, simply take note of the refrains to the psalms, I ask you, which in this place you sing not once, or two or three times, but many times, and you will take great consolation with you when you leave. [41] Take note, at any rate, of all the treasure the refrain itself opened up to you. Let no one tell me that before the commentary they did not recognise its force: even before the commentary the refrain is easily taken in by the listener who is at all interested in paying attention. I mean, if only you school yourself to say *As the deer longs for springs of water, so my soul longs for you, O God. My soul thirsted for God, who is strong and living: when shall I come and see the face of God?* even before the commentary you will be in a position to instil every sound value.

Not only this one, however: every refrain will provide us also with the same riches. If in turn you recite the verse "Blessed the man who fears the Lord," [42] you will also be in a position to see what it is you are saying: you will emulate not the rich man, not the official, not the handsome one, not the one blessed with good health, not the one with a splendid house, not the one with influence, not the one feted and feasted in palaces, no other such, but the one with piety, the one with sound values, the one with fear of God, not only with the future in mind but also with the present as well. [43] Here-below, after all, the latter is more influential than the former: if at some time disease strikes, the man in purple gets no benefit for relief of the ailment from bodyguards and much finery; instead, despite the presence of servants, family and everyone else, and despite being clad in layer upon layer of golden garments he is burning up with fever as though in a furnace. The man of pious life who fears God, on the contrary, with no parent or servant or anyone else in attendance, extinguished that furnace completely by raising his eyes to heaven not repeatedly but only two or three times. You could see the same thing happening in the circumstances and unexpected developments of life, the rich and famous alarmed, the people of piety and sound values bearing everything serenely. Aside from all this, even if no disaster occurred, the conscience of the person who fears God is full of deeper and purer satisfaction than the soul of the rich: the latter, even if giving the impression of enjoying the good life, feels worse than those living in hunger, recalling his troubles and living with a bad conscience, whereas the former, even if lacking necessary food, will be more cheerful than those enjoying the best of fare because nourished on sound expectations, and day in day out looks forward to the rewards of his good deeds.

Lest, however, I seem to bore you by prolonging the

sermon, (167) I shall leave the more studious to choose individual refrains and examine the force contained in them. [44] I shall thus close the sermon at this point by exhorting your good selves not to enter here to no effect, but to take up the refrains and make careful note of them as though they were pearls, meditate on them constantly at home and recite them all to your friends and your wives. Should suffering afflict you, should desire or anger or any other irrational passion excite you, sing them repeatedly, so that even in the present life we may enjoy great peace, and in the life to come attain the eternal goods, thanks to the grace and lovingkindness of our Lord Jesus Christ, to whom with the Father and the Holy Spirit be glory, power and honor, now and forever, for ages of ages. Amen.

First Homily on Psalm 49.16

On the verse of the prophet David,
"Do not be afraid when a person becomes rich, or when the glory
of their house is magnified,"[1] and on hospitality

While it is satisfying for a farmer to drive the plough to clear the pastures, dig the furrows, pull up the weeds and then sow the seed once no weeds are there to affect the sowing, it is much more satisfying to a speaker when he sows the divine thoughts among an audience that is free of disturbance. The reason that it is with satisfaction that we address ourselves to the sermon is that we see this pasture already cleared: though we do not see your mind, your eyes being open and hearing alert give me signs of the serenity within. [2] While, of course, I cannot intrude into your consciousness, your eyes being intent and uplifted convey the message that there is no disturbance within. Instead, you are on the contrary shouting with enthusiasm, Sow the seed, we welcome whatever you sow in the hope of a good crop, having expelled every earthly concern from our mind. Scripture, remember, requires not only a wise teacher but also an intelligent listener. Hence, while it is you I declare blessed, I bless also myself: "Blessed the one who speaks to listeners' ears," and "Blessed those who hunger and thirst after righteousness." [3]

We therefore sow the thoughts among you, who have come here with enthusiasm: while all the others are languishing in the marketplace with worldly concerns, you are elevated above the earth and receive the spiritual thoughts; while they are in thrall to the handmaid in waiting upon the flesh, you beautify the soul, which is noble and free, and attend to it. After all, where do you now spend your time, mortal that you are? In the marketplace. Amassing what kind of things? Slime and mire. Why go to the trouble of amassing money that perishes, covetousness that proves tyrannical, influence that perishes, a surfeit of earthly cares, here today (500) and gone tomorrow? Why pick the blooms and ignore the fruit? Why run after the shadow and not lay hold of the reality? Why chase what perishes and not seek what abides? "All flesh," after all, "is grass, and all human glory is the flower of grass; the grass withered, and the flower fell, whereas the word of the Lord abides forever." [4] You became rich? What good was this for your soul? The richer you became in money, the poorer in soul; you flourished in foliage and were lacking fruit. What good, tell me, is that? You acquired money, which you are destined to leave here-below; you acquired influence, which is the source of intrigue. Come hither, enjoy sentiments of great value, rid yourself of your sins, have done with your crimes, make your conscience pure, lift your thoughts on high, become angelic as well as human. Leave behind your fleshly nature and take up life's light wing, free yourself of visible things and depend on the invisible. Ascend to heaven, join the choir of angels, present yourself at the lofty tribunal on high. Leave behind smoke and shadow, grass and spider's webs – a term for such insignificance escapes me.

I repeat, and shall not cease saying it: Come in, prove yourself human lest you give the lie to your natural title. Do you understand what is said to you? He is a human being, someone may say, but a human being often in name only, not a human being in his way of thinking. I mean, when I see you living an irrational life, how am I to call you a human being and not an ox? when I see you robbing others, how am I to call you a human being and not a wolf? when I see you committing fornication, how am I to call you a human being and not a swine? when (501) I see you being fraudulent, how am I to call you a human being and not a serpent? when I see you with venom, how am I to call you a human being and not a snake? when I see you being a fool, how am I to call you a human being and not an ass? when I see you committing adultery, how am I to call you a human being and not a lusty stallion? when I see you disobedient and froward, how am I to call you a human being and not a stone?

You received nobility from God, why forfeit your natural virtue? Tell me, what are you doing? Other people have the skill to raise brute beasts, according to the locality, to the status of human beings, training parrots to produce a human voice, with their skill changing their nature, and making lions gentle and leading them through the marketplace: why do you turn a gentle lion into a wild animal and make yourself more fierce than a wolf? What is even worse is that while each brute beast has one failing, the wolf being rapacious, the serpent deceptive, the snake venomous, this is not the case with an evil human being: often it is not one failing the human being acquires, proving to be instead rapacious, deceptive, venomous, and acquiring in its own soul the vicious habits of the brute beasts.

How, then, do you call yourself human when you do not bear the insignia of royalty, when you do not wear the diadem, when you are not clothed in the purple? Scripture says, "Let us make a human being in our image and likeness."[5] Consider who it is of whom you have been made an image, human being, and do not descend to the level of brute beasts. If you see a king casting aside purple and diadem, mingling with the troops and forfeiting his own rank, how would you refer to such a king? You are a human being; so prove to me, not that you have a human soul, but whether you have a human way of thinking. You who control the brute beasts, have you become a slave to the brutish passions within you?

How, do you ask, am I to become a human being? If you keep the thoughts of the flesh under control, those brutish thoughts, if you expel lewd habits, if you expel an inopportune desire for money, if you expel that wicked tyrant, if you make your own place pure. But how do you become a human being? By coming here where human beings are created. If I receive you as a stallion, I turn you into a human being; if I receive you as a wolf, I turn you into a human being; if I receive you as a serpent, I turn you into a human being, not changing your nature but transforming your free will. But what are you saying? I have children, I run a house, I look after a wife, I am a victim of poverty, I am concerned for daily sustenance. These are excuses and pretexts: if I were to keep you here all the time and not allow you the slightest time to discharge your profane duties, you could mount a case to me claiming, I have children and I run a house, and you would be right do say so – or, rather, not even then ought you say this, since God is capable of arranging all your affairs for you in greater abundance while you are occupied here.

As it is, however, I put none of those obligations on you, I do not say, Spend time here each day – only twice a week. What is burdensome, what is demanding in that? Come to church, not for the whole day but for a short space of time. Adopt (502) spiritual thoughts so as not to incur wounds, with a view not to striking down others but to turning the marketplace into a church. Come in, take on armor so as with the armor to avoid the harmful blow; take your position in the battle lines provided you are wearing armor; take your position in a holy place provided your eyes are pure; enter port provided you are careful in sailing the ship. You can learn these skills in this place; if you are unwilling, you go into the world's fray without the protection of God's commandments. Consider what a great thing it is to leave the church scorning all human things, trampling on misfortune, proving superior to good fortune, neither carried away by the latter nor depressed by the former. Job was like that, neither overwhelmed by his poverty nor carried away with his wealth, but preserving equanimity amidst changing fortunes. [6]

Come in, take up armor from me. What sort of armor? The kind that guarantees you salvation. On leaving you will see a man mounted on a horse with a golden bridle, with many bodyguards around him, and in turn someone insignificant and abject. At that point, envy of the rich man assails you, malice towards the poor man grips you. David approaches you, stands at your side and says *Do not be afraid when a person becomes rich.* [7] Make your departure in the company of the prophet and do not be afraid; go off where I tell you with the prophet, with the teacher, with the staff, with the herald. *Do not be afraid when a person becomes rich.* But you will reply, This is to be expected of someone exhorting and advising and stating our duty; tell me also how it comes about that I do not need to be afraid of that person. Because the nature of riches resembles the nature of the human being; how that is, I shall tell you.

What is a human being? A lowly animal, mortal, short-lived. Riches are like that, too – or, rather, not like that but even less substantial: often they pass away, not with the human being, but even before the human being. You are aware of countless examples in this city of the untimely end of riches, and you have come to know that though the one possessing them is alive, the possession has gone, the end of riches meaning a change to poverty. Consider, therefore, how short-lived is possession: though the possessor is alive, the possession has gone; would that it alone had perished and not involved the possessor in ruin as well. You would therefore not be wrong to call riches an ungrateful servant, a bloodthirsty and murderous servant, a servant repaying his master with death.[8] And what is worse, it does not envelop him in perils when it leaves him: even before it leaves him, it alarms and disturbs him. I mean, have no eye for his vesture of silken garments, his smelling of myrrh and enjoying attendance on the outside: lay bare his conscience, reveal his mind even when he was rich, and inside you will see alarm and panic.

When you see another person falling victim to that fall, learn your own fate. I mean, what is more unreliable than human affairs? As I have often remarked, they resemble the condition of flowing rivers, at one time coming into view and flowing by, at another time checked and changing direction. *Do not be afraid when a person becomes rich.* (503) Adopt this verse, this spiritual song: when envy makes its appearance, and this verse also makes its appearance, the words eliminate the problem. *Do not be afraid when a person becomes rich.* This remedy of mine costs no money, only heaven: it is not the body I heal, I cure the soul – not yours alone, I mean, but mine as well.[9] After all, if I am a teacher, I am also human, subject to the same nature as yours, providing instruction applicable to us all. *Do not be afraid when a person becomes rich.* Adopt this verse as a treasure and a motto, adopt this verse as the root of wealth and affluence: real wealth is not being wealthy but not wishing to be wealthy. Have you understood what has been read to you?[10] The one wishing to be wealthy has need of possessions and money, whereas the one not wishing to be wealthy always enjoys affluence.

Do not be afraid when a person becomes rich, or when the glory of their house is magnified. Why, tell me, *do not be afraid*? Well, since those with riches can be fearsome, the inspired author divulges their life. Why be afraid of a person with luxuriant foliage but no fruit? why be afraid of person with bitter experiences? why be afraid of a person always trembling? why be afraid of a person living in constant fear? I mean, whereas your slave is not afraid when you are away, that person carries his master around within him: wherever he goes, the love of money follows. Neighbors, servants, friends, slanderers, benefactors – all alike he has as enemies, stirring up intense envy. You see, while a poor person lives without fear of anyone, being rich only in sound values and patience, the rich person, living a life of avarice, is hated by everyone and is surrounded by enemies in general assemblies, flattered to his face but hated in people's thinking.

Now, because this is the way things are, when the wind blows and dislodges the foliage, when a change in circumstances develops, then false friends show their true colors, then the demeanor of flatterers is shown for what it is worth, then the bevy of hypocrites is revealed, and the curtain is lifted on what is happening. Everyone's mouth opens with the cry, Villain, Criminal, Wretch! What are you saying? was it not only yesterday you were flattering him? were you not caressing his hands? That was all a charade: times have changed, the charade is over, I have shown my true colors. So why are you afraid, tell me, of the one criticised by so many? Why so? Would that he would criticise himself.

I say this to find fault, not with riches, as I have stated countless times, but with those who use a good thing badly; money is fine for good deeds. How is it fine? If they relieve indigence, if they set poverty to rights. Listen to how Job puts it: "I was an eye for the blind, a foot for the lame, I was a father to the powerless." See riches that involved not sin but love of the poor. "My house was open to allcomers." [11] This is the service of riches, riches not in name but in fact.

These riches are the slave of the other: one is riches in name only, bereft of facts, the other riches are real in name and fact. Of what kind are they? Riches of virtue, riches of almsgiving. In what way? I shall explain. There is a rich man who robs everyone's property, and there is a rich man who makes his property available to the poor: one is rich by amassing a fortune, the other by expending it; one tills the earth, (504) the other cultivates heaven. To the extent that heaven is superior to earth, the affluence of one pales before that of the other. One has countless friends, the other has everyone as critics.

What is really remarkable is that in the case of the avaricious thief not only the wronged but also those suffering nothing hate that evil person, sympathising with those who suffered abuse, whereas in the case of the almsgiver not only those receiving alms but also those who did not receive alms love him. Virtue, you see, brethren, is better than vice: vice has as its enemies even those not wronged, whereas almsgiving acquires as friends even those who are not the recipients of favors. Everyone, you see, says, God bless him! What favor did you, in fact, receive? I did not, but my brother did; I did not, but my fellow member did: the benevolence shown him I regard as shown me. Do you see what a great thing virtue is, how desirable, how lovable, how beautiful? The almsgiver is a haven to all, a father to all, a staff for the aged. In the case of the almsgiver, if he meets with misfortune, everyone prays for him, God have mercy on him, may he treat him well, may good things abide with him, whereas if it happens to the robber, you will hear them say, Villain, Criminal, Blackguard! What wrong did you do? I did none, it was my brother. [12] Countless cries day in day out. If he stumbles, everyone is on him. Is this life? is this riches? is this not worse than a condemned criminal? The criminal surrenders his life, this man his soul. Do you see him in bonds and not pity him? The reason I hate him is that he is bound not by necessity but by choice – hence his attracting the chains.

Are you against riches once again? they will reply to me. For your part you are once more against the poor. Are you against the robbers once again? For your part are you once more against the robbed? [13] You for your part never tire of eating and biting the poor to pieces, and I never tire of setting you right. Are you always attached to them? are you always attached to the poor? Get away from my sheep, get away from my flock, do it no harm. If you harm my flock, will you charge me with going after you? If I were shepherd of the flock, would you charge me with going after a wolf that is attacking the flock? I am shepherd of the rational nurslings: [14] I go after you not with stones but with words – or, rather, instead of going after you, I call to you, Be a sheep, come hither, become part of the fold. Why do you harm the flock when you ought build up the fold? It is not you I go after: I go after a wolf; if you are not a wolf, I am not going after you – but if you turn wolf, I blame you.

I am not against the rich: I am in favor of the poor. In saying so, I am speaking for your good, even if you do not realise it. How am I speaking for your good? Because I rid you of sin, I free you from robbery, I make you friends of everyone, attractive to everyone. I have always said to you, Did you rob? did you practise avarice? Come in, and I shall change you, I shall change hostility into friendship, danger into security. This I do here-below, and up there I give you further the kingdom of heaven so that you may not depart into unending punishments, but lay hold of good things "which eye has not seen nor ear heard, nor has it entered the human heart." [15] Is this, then, the action of one pursuing you, or one giving you (505) good advice? the action of one who loves you or one who hates you? No, you hate me. No, I love you; I have a command from the Lord, "Love your enemies." So as to heal you, I do not keep my distance from you. Our Lord was crucified and said, "Forgive them, Father: they do not know what they are doing." [14]

Surely I am not persecuting you? I am driving out your ailment. Surely it is not you I am attacking? It is your vices. Do you not consider me a benefactor? do you not find me caring? do you not take me for a protector ahead of all others? who else will speak to you of these things? will the magistrate? Nothing of the kind – only charges and prosecution. Your wife? only talk of finery and gold. [15] Your son? only talk of inheritance, wills, bequests. Your servant? only talk of service, slavery, freedom. Toadies? Only talk of parties, feasts, meals. People at the theatre? Only vile jokes and talk of unfettered lust. People in court? only talk of contracts, inheritance, freedom, crimes committed. Where are you able to hear about these things if not from me? Everyone is afraid of you, I despise you; as long as you are in this condition I despise you, I scorn you, I despise your ailment. I cut, you scream – but I am not put off by your cries, I only long for your salvation, being a surgeon, after all. Surely if you have an ulcer and call for a surgeon, and you see him sharpening the knife, you say, Make the incision even if I am in agony, since you look for recovery from that incision. But you shun me though I make no incision, only purging your mind by word. Yet what does the surgeon do? He cuts many times and makes the ulcer worse, whereas I make you not worse but better. In his rooms, you see, nature is at a loss, and remedies powerless, whereas here there is the power of language. A surgeon does not guarantee you recovery, but I guarantee you recovery: listen to me. [16] This is the reason the only-begotten Son of God came down, to bring us up and place us above the heavens.

One thing alone I am afraid of: sin; have done with all the rest, be they riches, poverty, power, or anything else. This I say, and shall not cease saying it: I want none of my fold to perish. What, then? is it possible for a rich person to be saved? Certainly: Job was rich, Abraham was rich. Did you take note of his wealth? Have an eye also for his hospitality. Did you take note of the table he laid? Have an eye also for his friendliness. So what of Abraham? He was rich; surely I do not have to convince you of this? was Abraham rich? Yes, he was rich. Did you take note of his wealth? Have an eye also for his lifestyle. At midday the Lord appeared to him when he was sitting by the oak tree at Mamre: behold, there were three men. He got up (not thinking it was God who was there: how could he?), bowed low and said, If you think me worthy, take shelter under my roof. [17] Did you take note of what the old man was doing at midday? Instead of staying under cover, he extended a pressing invitation to strange travelers who were utterly unknown to him. The rich and noble man got up and bowed low; the man of affluence left his house, wife, children, servants; despite having three hundred and eighteen of them, [18] he left them all and went out to make a catch, he cast his net of hospitality, lest any traveler or stranger pass by his house. See what the old man does: he does not give instructions to a servant, though (506) having three hundred and eighteen of them, knowing that servants by and large are lazy, the risk being that the servant might take a nap and the stranger would pass by and he would miss his catch.

Take note of Abraham, take note of the rich man. For your part, do you deign even to acknowledge a poor man, even to reply to him, even to converse with him? Even if you ever give him something, it is through a slave. The good man was not like this, however; on the contrary, he sat there and put up with the hot sun, perspiring with the heat. The desire for hospitality was shade for him; he sat eating the fruit of hospitality, despite being rich. Compare him, I ask you, with rich people today: where do they sit at midday? In hell. Where do they sit? In the death of drunkenness. Where do they sit? In the public eye, dissolute, drunk, hearts blinded, more brutish than brute beasts. The good man was not like that. Would you like to imitate Abraham? Imitate him, then: far from hindering you, I urge you, though more is required of us than of Abraham: "If your righteousness does not exceed that of the scribes and pharisees," Scripture says, "you will not enter the kingdom of heaven." [19] For the time being, however, at least reach the standard of Abraham.

He was hospitable, he got up and bowed low, unaware of who the visitors were; had he been aware, his attending on God would not have been a remarkable thing for him to do. His ignorance of the visitors' identity, however, puts in a stronger light his zeal for hospitality. He sat and he gave welcome. In what way? Generously: he killed a calf, he calls Sarah as well and makes his wife a sharer in his hospitality, not hidden away in her chamber but standing by the oak. That meal, in fact, then opened her womb and corrected the barrenness of nature. He killed a calf and received Isaac, he mixed flour and received its seed like the stars of heaven and the sand of the sea. [20] But you will surely respond, Give me also a crop of so many fine children. Miserable and vile wretch, do you seek what is on earth? I give you heaven, life with the angels, enjoyment for eternity, and you seek death and corruption? I give you life without end – a greater reward, a fuller recompense.

Give careful attention to what I say so as to see the reversal of fortunes: when he had to show hospitality, what did Abraham say to his wife Sarah? "Hurry, mix three measures of fine flour." [21] Let women listen to what is said: "Hurry, mix three measures of fine flour." The spectacle is for us all, and the classroom is open to both sexes: [22] let women listen to what is said, let men also listen and imitate. "Hurry," the text says, "mix three measures of fine flour," and he ran to the herd of cattle. They divide the labor so as to divide also the crown. Married life is in common; let the works of virtue also be in common. I received you as a helpmate; [23] be a helpmate to me also in higher things. Hurry, hurry: he urges his wife on lest delay displease the guests. "Hurry, mix three measures (507) of fine flour." Demanding the direction, burdensome the order: "Mix three measures of fine flour." She did not retort, What? did I marry you with the expectation that you would turn me, your wife with so much wealth, into a miller and baker? do you have three hundred and eighteen slaves, and instead of choosing to give them orders, you give me this job? She did not say anything of the sort, nor did she think it; instead, since she was Abraham's wife, not only by a relationship of body but also by a sharing in virtue, hence he says, "Hurry, mix," knowing his wife's devotion.

Where are the wives of today? Let us compare them to Sarah. Surely they do not accept such orders, such tasks? Extend to me the hand of the wife in her finery, and you see it gilded on the outside but inside under siege. How many poor people's impoverishment, tell me, does your hand carry? Extend your hand to me, show it to me: what is it wearing? Greed. Extend the hand of Sarah: what is it wearing? Hospitality, almsgiving, love, care of the poor. What a lovely arm! Consider one arm and the other: each has the appearance of an arm, but the differences are immense – in one case floods of tears, in the other wreaths and trophies. I say this so that women may not look for such things from their husbands, and husbands not accede to their wives' requests for such things. Look at Sarah, look at the rich woman mixing three measures of fine flour. How much effort was involved? She did not notice the effort, however, on account of her expectation of fruit and profit. "Hurry, mix three measures of fine flour."

What are you up to? titivating yourself, woman? to please whom – your husband? False devotion if this is the way you aim to please your husband, if this is the way you hurry to please your husband. So how am I to please him? With modesty. Still, how am I to please him? With simplicity, with sound values, with gentleness and love, with fellow-feeling and harmony. These are your adornments, woman; these virtues of yours produce fellow-feeling, whereas those other adornments do not succeed in pleasing, but even cause you to be burdensome to your husband. When in fact you say, Lay hold of it and bring it to me, you may be pleasing for a while, but later you will have an enemy. For you to learn, however, that it is not your husband you are pleasing – in fact, at home you take them off, and in church you wear them; if you were out to please your husband, you would wear them at home – but as I said, you come into church with hands and neck covered in gold. If Paul enters, that fearsome and welcome figure – fearsome to sinners, welcome to pious people – he cries aloud in these terms, "It becomes women to deck themselves out, not in gold, not in pearls, not in richly woven clothing." [24] Then if a pagan enters and sees those women so decked out up above, and down below Paul saying this, will he not comment, It is all show and make-believe? It is not show on our part, even if this happens in that fashion; but the pagan suffers injury and says, I went into a Christian church and heard Paul saying, "Not in gold and in pearls," but it gave the opposite impression in practice.

What use is gold to you, woman? to appear lovely (508) and charming? But it contributes nothing to your beauty of soul. Be attractive in your soul, and you will be desirable also in body. "A person's wisdom will light up their countenance," [25] though wisdom belongs to their soul. Nothing so creates longing and desire as love: if your husband loves you, even if you are ugly, you will be desirable to him, whereas if he hates you, even if you are beautiful, he will have no wish to see you. Hatred in the soul, you see, does not allow the beauty of the face to appear: when you are on the point of asking him for adornments and gold, he is then on the point of hating and shunning you like a beggar in the marketplace; while he cannot shun him, however, he can you, since you are constantly at home, asking for attention that is unreasonable. Far from simply giving heed to this, woman, let your mind also be changed. My words are drastic remedies – drastic at the time but consistently cheering. I am a surgeon, I prod your sores in case they get more entrenched and spread further: while I provide treatment and grant you healing through words, others exemplify the passing, deceitful and despicable character of the present life. But let every woman inscribe on her mind what I said about Abraham (not forgetting the promise), "Hurry and mix," let each man have it on his conscience.

Why, I ask you, do you wear silken garments, ride horses with golden bridles and mules all dolled up? A mule is dolled up underneath, the gold is kept under cover, mules unendowed with reason carry money around and have golden bridles, mules unendowed with reason are dolled up, while the poor person wasting with hunger sits at your door, and Christ wastes with hunger. What utter nonsense! what excuse is there for it? how forgive it, when Christ stands before your doors in the guise of a poor person, and you are utterly unmoved? who will save you from punishment for it? I gave an alms, you say. But don't give only what the person wishes: give as much as you can. What will you say, tell me, at the time when the unbearable punishments, when that awful retribution, the threats, the fearsome power, when the river of fire boils up, when the fearsome tribunal, when the impartial judgement, when the nature that has no beginning, when lack of human resources, when neither mother nor father, no neighbor, no king, no wayfarer nor stranger can help you? Standing alone with your deeds, will you be condemned by them or crowned by them? What will you say then? You will remember my words then – but what good will they be to you? None: when the rich man likewise also remembered and looked for an opportunity for repentance, it was all to no avail. Yet he insisted, "Send Lazarus to dip the tip of his finger in water and cool my tongue, because I am in terrible pain."[26] He did not send

Lazarus, however, not because the mighty stream of paradise would miss a single drop, but because a sprinkling of mercy would make no impression on harshness: since at the time of the contest he was scorned, at the time of the awards he accorded him no consolation.

I tell you this, not for the poor person to lament his poverty, (509) nor for the rich man to rejoice in his wealth. Are you well off? Riches would perish unless you made the due amount available. "Hurry and mix three measures of fine flour." Then he ran to the cattle and killed a calf. The old man turned runner: far from his bodily vigor being spent, his sense of sound values was heightened, enthusiasm overcame nature; the master of three hundred and eighteen servants carried the calf without being troubled by the weight, his mind lightened by his enthusiasm. The old man was faced with the running and the attentive service, and his wife with the hard work: they lavished on the guests not only a generous amount of money and a well-furnished table, but also attentive ministry and service, attending to them not through their servants but with their own hands and limbs. Then the wife stood by in the role of a servant, and the guests reclined, unrecognised. I shall not stop short of recounting it: they thought they were some poor people, but instead of worrying about that, they welcomed them as guests. They both stood by at that time, reaping the harvest of hospitality in their attitude, their sound values, their service, their welcome, their labor, their ministry, their love, their arrangements, their careful attention, leaving nothing to chance. The wife stood by the tree, using the tree for an inner chamber, with the cover of the leaves for shade, and was not ashamed to be in public; she stood there with her innate decorum on show, gathering the fruit of her service. So what did the visitor say? "I shall return in good time, and Sarah will have a son." [27] What fruit the meal produced! how wonderful! how swift! how timely! what a ripe and mature fruit! That statement, you see, entered the womb and created the child. Such are the fruits of hospitality.

Pay attention to what I am going to say. Later, when the child grew up, the one born of the meal, when the fruit of hospitality became a man (it was not so much the womb that produced it as the meal, though the word of God before everything else), when he grew up and became a man, and it was time for marriage – pay careful attention to what I am saying – that old man, blessed Abraham the patriarch, was then about to die. Now, he was living as a stranger among depraved women and a most wicked nation; so he called his servant and said, How wicked the Canaanite women are. So what do you want? Go off to the land where I was born, and bring a wife from there for my son. [28] Unusual and unexpected arrangements. You are aware and understand perfectly that when someone wants to get a wife for their son, father and mother discuss it, visit other people's house, flattering one, complimenting another, with plenty of matchmakers, bridal attendants, promise of dowries; father and mother anxiously discuss it amongst themselves, no shame, no reserve, leaving nothing to servants, whereas when a guest comes, Go and bring him inside and entertain him. [29] With Abraham, on the other hand, it was the reverse: when he had a task to perform (510) that was important and called for sound values, he did it himself, entrusting hospitality not to a servant but to his wife and himself. But when arrangements were to be made for a wife and a marriage, he says to a servant, Off you go. In our day women do the opposite: if they want to talk to a goldsmith, they are not ashamed to go off on their own and sit nearby in case the gold be stolen, love of money allowing them to lose their sense of shame and dignity. Abraham was not like that, however: when he wanted to welcome guests, he and his wife did it personally; but when it was marriage, he did it through his servant.

Why mention Abraham, then? Because he was rich. Think

of this about Abraham in your case, too, and you will never scorn anyone. But at what point did we digress to say these things? We were citing the inspired author and his staff, *Do not be afraid when a person becomes rich*: it was that verse that prompted all this; and, see, we found a treasure full of gold. *Do not be afraid when a person becomes rich.*[30] Take this staff, which is capable of steadying trembling bodies: it is not so much in the nature of a staff to steady trembling bodies of the aged and infirm as this verse stirs up the mind of young and old trembling with lust and beset by sin. *Do not be afraid when a person becomes rich* Why be in dread of a human being, human as he is and not a wolf? why be in dread of a human being awash with godlessness and covered in gold? why be in dread of a human being betrayed by his own iniquity, often with his enemy within?

The prophet, however, made it clear to me when he said *Do not be afraid when a person becomes rich.* Tell me now also how it is that I should not be afraid of the rich man. *Or when the glory of his house is magnified.* What nobility of expression! how well he introduced sound values in his description and teaching. *Do not be afraid when a person becomes rich, or when the glory of his house is magnified.* He did not say, When his glory is magnified, but *the glory of his house.* You see, when you enter the house of a rich man and see in his home pillars rising to a great height, golden capitals, marble overlays on the wall, flowing springs and fountains, covered walkways, trees swaying in the wind, everything covered in mosaics, a herd of golden-clad eunuchs, a crowd of servants, carpets on the floor, a table glowing with gold, decorated chambers – all this is the glory of the house, not the glory of the person.[31] A persons' glory, after all, is piety, simplicity, almsgiving, gentleness, humility, peace, righteousness, genuine love for all – all these constitute a person's glory. Why are you afraid of the rich? Fear rather his house, therefore: it is rich, not the occupant. But I am not afraid of it, you say. Why? Because the gold is inanimate material. Yet you are afraid of the human being? Yes. Why? surely the riches are not his? The splendor belongs to the house, it is the wall that has marble on it – so what of the occupant? It is the ceiling that is of gold – so what of its owner? The capitals (511) of the pillars are of gold – so what of his head smeared with sin? Is the floor clean? His conscience is unclean. Are his garments silken? His soul is covered in rags. The house is rich, but the house's owner is poor.

When the glory of his house is magnified. For you to learn that it is the house's glory, not the person's, I challenge you from your own words. Often when you enter someone's house that is beautiful, what do you say on entering? I saw beautiful marble. Surely you do not say, I saw a beautiful person? The pillars are marvelous, the windows lovely. Surely you do not say, The occupant is marvelous? There is much gold on the ceiling. Surely you do not say, There is much almsgiving? There are many fountains and much lavishness. Surely you do not say, There is a lavish display of that owner? You are speaking in every case of the walls, in every case of the marble, in every case of the fountains, in every case of the flowing springs. As well you see a horse with a golden bridle, and you say, The bridle is lovely, the compliment being for the goldsmith. A wonderful garment, the commendation going to the weaver. Excellent servants, the commendation going to the trader. The person remains without recognition, the things surrounding him enjoying the plaudits. When you see a person, on the other hand, you say, Fine fellow, charming, kind, admirable, charitable, benevolent, contrite, always attending to his prayers, always observing the fast, always spending time in church, always attached to the divine teaching. These are the compliments to him, this the recognition.

Learn, therefore, what are the riches of a person, what the riches of a house, and *Do not be afraid*: if you learn to distinguish the riches properly, you will no longer be afraid.

Now, do you recognise that the one considered rich by you is really poor and needy? *Do not be afraid when a person becomes rich.* For you to learn that this is the way things are, even if here-below you have the wrong impression, consider him at the moment of death. Surely (512) he does not take any of this to that place as he passes on? At that time the one who was clad in silken garments is dead and lies naked; he lies naked on the ground, the servants come and go, and none spares him a thought, not being his servants, after all. He passes on, and from now on nothing of him remains. [32] His wife is distraught, she undoes her hair; everyone consoles here, she does not respond. The children are orphaned, the wife widowed, everyone is abject – cupbearers, stewards, toadies, flatterers, eunuchs. To take some of those vessels and make off with them is beyond him: why? He is carried off by himself. They deliver panegyrics: what good is it to him this time? does vainglory give him a good reputation? Why? Surely he cannot take anything from it? Nothing of it can accompany him on that day. The one who laid his hands on everything goes off to the grave, is buried in three cubits, and is no more; earth lies on his face, the grave his shroud, and his wife departs.

Where are his riches? where his slaves? where the pomp and circumstance? where the huge and many-splendored house? They have deserted him; even his wife leaves him, albeit unwillingly, the stench driving her off, the floods of maggots pursuing her. Is that all? Yes, he passed on with nothing of his own. For you to learn that he passed on with nothing of his own, we do not take leave of the tomb of the blessed martyrs since they receive what is due to them. In the former case not even the wife can bring herself to stay, whereas in the latter case the emperor casts off his crown and stays at the tomb of the martyr, troubled in countenance and begging to be given release from his crimes and victory against the enemy. [33]

Do not be afraid when a person becomes rich. Taking up this verse, let us begin a hymn to the Lord, giving thanks for all this to him, Father, Son and Holy Spirit, because to him belong the glory and the power for ages of ages. Amen.[34]

Second Homily on Psalm 49.16

The homily was delivered in Constantinople in the Great Church after someone else spoke, with few assembled, on the verse, "Do not be afraid when a person becomes rich," and on almsgiving[1]

Of brief duration but ripe the fruit of the excellent speaker, delicate the chord but resounding the note, brief the words but rich the thoughts. In fact, he set the whole body agog with his compliments, made them more enthusiastic with his praise, pointed to the one responsible for the cultivation, and by both composing hymns to him and giving thanks according to the apostolic norm[2] he concluded his words with a doxology. Now, if he was brisk in laying the table, it was due not to poverty but to humility: far from being at a loss for more to say when he brought his words to an end, he yielded the role of teaching to us.

So, come now, let us also, now that we are rid of the tempest of the recent hubbub,[3] cleanse our hearing with the reading of the Scriptures as though with a kind of river water. This is what sailors do, too: after they run through a storm and put in at a peaceful haven after crossing a large ocean, they loosen the sail, remove the oar, disembark, rejuvenate the body with baths, food and drink, sleep and recreation, and thus make it more vigorous for sailing in the future. Let us, too, imitate them, and (513) rid of the uproar, disturbance and billows of recent days, put our soul in at the reading of the Scriptures as though into some peaceful harbor.[4] It is, after all, a harbor without billows, an impregnable wall, an unshakeable tower, imperishable glory, invulnerable armor, imperturbable satisfaction, undying enjoyment and whatever else you class as good – such is the communion with the divine Scriptures. It repels discouragement, preserves good spirits, makes the poor person richer than the affluent, bestows security on the rich, makes the sinner righteous, sets a secure guard on the righteous, snatches away ill-gotten gains, makes goods that are missing spring up, drives out wickedness, leads on to virtue – or does not so much lead on as even roots deeply and makes it last without end, being a spiritual remedy, a kind of divine and ineffable incantation which eliminates ailments, rooting up the thorns of sin, making the furrow clean, casting the seeds of piety and bringing the crop to fruition.

Let us not disregard such wonderful goods, let us not be absent from assemblies; instead, let us betake ourselves here on a regular basis so that we may receive constant healing, and no one on seeing a rich person may be smitten with envy or distressed by poverty.[5] Rather, let them learn the true nature of things, and bypass the shadow to cling fast to the reality: a shadow, even if seeming to be larger than the body, is nevertheless only a shadow; it is larger in no other way than appearance, and it appears to be at the time we are farther from the sun's rays – for example, at midday, when the sun is directly overhead, it shrinks in every direction, is reduced and becomes smaller. You can see this happening also in human affairs: the further you distance yourself from virtue, the more important seem the affairs of the present life; but when you place yourself in the bright light of the Scriptures, then you recognise the insignificance, brevity and nothingness of these passing affairs, and you gain a clear knowledge that they are nothing better than river currents, appearing and passing on at the one time.[6]

This is the reason that the inspired author delivers a corrective to mean-spirited and wretched people, crawling on the ground and hankering after the mirage of wealth, in fear and trembling at those who abound in it. To deliver us from such anguish and convince us to scorn such things as of no value, he said *Do not be afraid when a person becomes rich, or when the glory of his house is magnified, because when he dies he will take none of it.* Do you see the precision of the expression and very clear distinction? He did not say, note, When his glory is magnified, but *the glory of his house*, to bring out that a person's glory is one thing, the glory of his house another. What, then, is a person's glory, and what the glory of his house? It is, after all, necessary to get a clear knowledge of this so as not to embrace dreams in place of the truth. The glory of a house, then, are porticos, covered walkways, ceilings of gold, a mosaic floor, lawns, gardens, herds of slaves, rich furniture, none of which applies to the person.[7] A person's glory is orthodox faith,[8] zeal as God wishes, love, gentleness, simplicity, (514) devotion in prayer, generosity in almsgiving, chastity, modesty and all the other aspects of virtue. To be sure that these are the forms they take: the one possessing them does not reap glory from them, nor would you be called beautiful if you had a beautiful house, garden, lawn, crowd of servants or richness of apparel; all the admiration remains with the possession, not passing to the owner. In other words, we admire the house, garden, lawn and beauty of attire, which is a compliment to the skill of the artisans, not to the virtue of the owner – on the contrary, it is proof of their vicious ways.

At any rate, it is so far from being the truth that owners of possessions are naturally endowed with glory that it runs an extreme risk of being undermined. In fact, everyone represents those displaying a surfeit of these things as cruel, inhumane, ignoble and opposed to sound values, these things being not a person's glory, as I said, but the glory of the house. It is those, on the contrary, who are living a life of temperance, modesty, gentleness, simplicity, and are earnestly devoted to God whom we admire, commend and proclaim, for the reason that this is a person's glory. Aware of this, therefore, believe no one to be devoted who is invested with those things that have nothing in common with him. Even if you should see someone seated on a chariot, eyebrows raised, erect, aspiring to the very clouds – not from the nature of things (impossible, in fact), but from the soul's derangement, or rather stupidity – do not think he enjoys a high reputation or is exalted and important: it is not mules in harness that make you exalted, but the pinnacle of virtue that leads you to the vault of heaven. Even if you espy someone else mounted on a horse, with many attendants clearing people before him in the marketplace, instead of declaring him blessed on that score disclose the condition of his soul, and then make a judgement on him on the basis of what that vision suggests. [9]

How ridiculous are the things visible to us on the surface! I mean, tell me, why clear the way before you in the marketplace? why push out of the way those you meet, and shun human beings, being one yourself? What conceit! what nonsense! Surely you have not turned into a wolf or a lion, to enter a city and put everyone to flight? Rather, even a wolf would not ever drive off a wolf, or a lion a lion, but mix with them out of respect for commonality of nature; but you, who have many other reasons along with nature for mildness, humility, equality, why do you become wilder than the wild beasts, and out of an unreasonable attitude spurn reasonable beings? Whereas your Lord brought the human being up to heaven, do you not even mix with him in the marketplace? Why mention heaven? Whereas he is seated on a royal throne, do you drive him even from the city? What is it to you that the bridle decorating the horse has to be of gold? what pretext or what excuse do you have for titivating excessively a brute beast that has no appreciation of extravagance (whether gold or lead makes no difference to it) while you see Christ wasting with hunger and do nothing to have him enjoy basic necessities? Why do you shrink from mingling with human beings, being one yourself, and instead look for isolation in the middle of cities, not considering that your Lord ate with tax collectors, (515) spoke with a prostitute, was crucified with brigands, and mingled with people? Instead, obsessed with conceit and folly, you forfeit even being human.

From this springs your great neglect of almsgiving, from this your inclination to avarice, from this your cruelty and inhumanity: when you fit the horse with a golden bridle, your servant with a golden armlet, stones with gold leaf, when the skins you have are of gold, clothing of gold, a belt and sandals of gold, and you impose on yourself such necessity for this wickedness out of a wish to satisfy insatiable lust and feed the wildest beast of all – I mean greed – then it is that you divest orphans, strip widows, go about as an enemy to everyone, set on a course that is futile and a direction that has no worthwhile outcome. I mean, what reason is there for you to have a gilded savage as your servant? what value is there in it? what good for your soul? what help to your body? what sort of introduction to your house? Quite the contrary: absurd expense, an outlay reeking of stupidity, a basis for licentiousness, a schooling in vice, an occasion for crude and promiscuous living, ruination of the soul, a way leading to countless evils.[10] Couches inlaid with silver, gold-spangled, footstools and basins made of the same material, loud laughter – how does that help you get your life in order? what improvement did that do to you, or your partner, or anyone else in the house? Is it not this that encourages brigands and burglars? is it not this that encourages servants to make off? You see, when they notice silver gleaming everywhere, the idea of theft enters their head; after all, if silver shining in the marketplace attracts you to lust, free as you are and boasting of your noble birth, much more a servant. I say this, not to acquit of blame runaway servants committing such crimes, but to urge you not to provide them with food for such thoughts.

Are we to dispose of these things? you ask. Are we to bury

them in the ground? Far from it; but if you do not mind my advice, I shall tell you a way to enable you to make the runaway grateful. It is wealth, you see, that is the runaway, here today and gone tomorrow – and not only a runaway, but also a maker of runaways, often turning its guards into fugitives. [11] So how would this runaway be held in check? In the opposite way to the other runaways: while they stay put if watched over, this takes flight when watched over, but stays if let loose. Now, if the saying strikes you as novel, learn its truth from farmers: if they shut the grain up in the house and bury it, they lose it by surrendering it to worm and maggot, whereas if they scatter it in the furrows, not only do they keep it but they also turn it into more. Wealth likewise, if staying in coffers under lock and key or even put in a hole in the ground, swiftly make off, whereas if you cast it into the belly of the poor in the manner of the farmer casting the seed into the furrow, it will not only not make off but thereby even become more abundant.

Aware of this, then, do not surrender it to a servant, but cause it to be held in countless hands, those of widows, of orphans, of the maimed, of those in prison: (516) it could not escape such a grasp, but would be held securely and become more abundant. What, you ask, am I to leave to my children? I do not actually oblige you to divest yourself of everything; but even if it were everything, you would make them the better off for it, bequeathing to them a propitious God in place of money, an affluence from almsgiving, countless supporters and benefactors even among human beings. You see, just as we hate the avaricious, even if we are not their victims, so we respect and are fond of those in the habit of giving alms, even if we do not personally benefit from their generosity – and not only them but also their children. Consider, therefore, how comely it would be for your children to have countless admirers if your wealth were spent on the support of the needy, all saying these words, The child of a kind man, The child of a generous man. In your own case, while you are idly and to no purpose titivating some unappreciative thing – stone being unappreciative even if you overlay it with countless talents of gold – you fail to share even basic necessities with the appreciative person wasting with hunger.

When that fearsome tribunal appears, therefore, and the rivers of fire, [12] and we are called to account for our doings, what will you say on such stupidity, on such folly and cruelty and inhumanity? What persuasive excuse will you offer? After all, as there is a purpose and a reason for everyone else – the farmer, if called to account, will say why he yoked oxen, ploughed furrows, and steered the plough, and the merchant why he launched the ship, hired workers and invested money, and the builder, the shoemaker, the smith, the baker and the tradesman of every kind will give an account and an explanation – so too you, enveloping the couch with silver and the horse and stone with gold, and preparing skins of this kind, what explanation will you give when called to account? what tack will you adopt? Is your sleep any sweeter on such a couch? You would not be in a position to say, however; rather, paradoxically speaking, it is even more restless: the worry is greater, and the anguish keener. Is the building more secure for its gold? Not even this is true. Is the horse better for its bridle? the servant? Quite the contrary in this case, too.

So why do you betray so much vulgarity in all these things? You will doubtless reply that they make your glory more splendid. Then did you not hear at the beginning of the sermon that these things do not constitute a person's glory, [13] but rather on the contrary they bring dishonor and reproach, criticism and mockery? From them spring envy and slander and countless other evils; and the more lasting the possessions, the more persistent the criticism. These large and magnificent houses stand there giving voice, even after the owners' death, as the most trenchant of critics; whereas the body is consigned to the earth, the sight of the dwellings does not permit the memory of the greed to be interred with the flesh. Instead, every bystander with eyes on the height and size of the large and magnificent house will say either to themselves or to the neighbor, (517) On what awful tears this house was built! how many orphans robbed! how many widows wronged! how many people deprived of their due! And so the opposite result befalls you: in your wish to enjoy glory in your lifetime, even at the end of your life you are not rid of critics; instead, the house bruits abroad your name as though inscribed on a bronze pillar, and causes countless people who never even saw you when alive to hurl taunts at you.

Since this lavish outlay does not bring even this advantage, then, let us avoid, dearly beloved, let us avoid the ailment, and not become wilder than the brute beasts. Everything is held in common by them – earth, springs, pastures, mountains, glens – and none has more than another, whereas though you are a human being, the mildest of living things, you become worse than a wild beast and swallow up in a single house the resources of countless poor people many times over. [14] In fact, it is not only our nature that is common to us, but also many more things than our nature – sky, sun and moon, the mass of stars, air and sea, fire and water and earth, life and death, growth and old age, sickness and health, the need for nourishment and clothing. Likewise spiritual goods are common – this sacred table, the body of the Lord, the precious blood, the promise of the kingdom, the bath of regeneration, the cleansing of sins, righteousness, holiness, redemption, the ineffable goods "that eye has not seen nor ear heard, nor has it entered the human heart." [15] So how could it not be absurd for those who (518) share so many things with one another – nature, grace, promises, laws – to be so greedy for money as not to maintain the same equality and exceed the wildness of brute beasts, despite being destined shortly after to leave them, and not simply leave them but even for their sake to put at risk their ultimate salvation? Death, you see, snatches them from enjoyment and then conducts them to examination and to undying punishments.

To avoid this happening, therefore, let us practise much almsgiving: it is the queen of virtues, which encourages us to appear there with confidence and rescues us from retribution and punishment, no one objecting to the person entering heaven in its company: its wing is light, of a high order the confidence it inspires, and it ascends to the very throne of the king, ushering in its devotees without fear. "Your prayers and your alms ascended as a memorial before God," Scripture says, remember. [16] Why, then, are we also not to ascend to that height, rid of this untimely avarice, useless luxury and extravagance? Let us make idle things useful, sending that wealth ahead and entrusting it to the right hand of the judge, who will guard it carefully and on the day of judgement will for that reason prove mild and propitious. Even if we are guilty of many sins, he will grant us pardon and the opportunity for defence. May this be the good fortune of us all, thanks to the grace and lovingkindness of Jesus Christ our Lord, to whom be the glory and the power for ages of ages. Amen.

Homily on Psalm 146.1

Delivered in Holy Week, including an explanation
of why it is called Holy Week.
On the verse, "Praise the Lord, O my soul!"
And on the prison in Acts.

We have completed the voyage of fasting, and thanks to God's grace we have now entered port. Let us, however, not grow indifferent on account of entering port, [1] but rather be zealous on account of reaching the end. This, remember, is what pilots also do: when they are on the point of bringing into the mouth of the port a heavily-laden merchantman full of grain and other cargo stacked high, they are anxious and apprehensive lest after the lengthy voyage the ship strike a rock and lose all the merchandise right there. This should be our concern and anxiety, too, lest we fall at the stage of the rewarding of our labors; hence we should even intensify our zeal. This is what runners also do: when they see themselves getting close to the tape, it is then they particularly increase the pace. This is what fighters also do, despite countless bouts and countless victories, exerting themselves particularly at the time they get close to the crown, and increasing their enthusiasm. [2]

Let us now do likewise: what port is for pilots, the tape for runners and crowns for fighters, this is what this week is for us, the summit of good things, and the title fight. [3] Hence we also call it Great, not because its days have a longer span than all the others – in fact, in this week the long drawn out tyranny of the devil is brought to an end, death is extinguished, the strong man bound, his accoutrements snatched from him, sin done away with, the curse abolished, paradise opened, heaven made accessible, human beings mingling with angels, the dividing wall broken down, the barrier removed, the God of peace making peace between things above and things on earth. [4] This is the reason the week is called Great; and just as it is the chief of all the weeks, so its summit is Holy Saturday; just as the head is to the body, so is Saturday to the week.

Hence in it we heighten our zeal: some people redouble their fasting, some their sacred vigils, some practise more generous almsgiving, testifying by their zeal for good works and the heightened piety of their life the magnitude of the benefaction conferred on us by God. Just as when the Lord raised Lazarus, remember, everyone in Jerusalem came out to meet him (520) and testified by the large numbers that he had raised a corpse to life (the interest of those leaving the city being proof of the marvel), [5] so too the current interest in this Holy Week also is a sign of the magnitude of the deeds occurring in it: everyone comes out to meet Christ today, not just from one city nor from Jerusalem alone – rather, from the whole world countless churches come from all parts to meet Jesus, not holding and waving palm branches, but offering to Christ the Lord alms, kindness, virtue, fasting, tears, prayers, vigils and piety of all kinds.

Now, it is not ourselves only who honor this week; instead, as well the emperors of our world have honored it in no perfunctory manner by giving a holiday to everyone involved in the city's community affairs so that they may thus enjoy the leisure and devote all these days to the spiritual services. Hence they also closed the doors of the courts: Let every civil case be held over, went the decree, every kind of dispute and retribution, and let the hands of the executioners take a short rest. The Lord's deeds are for all to celebrate: let something good be done also by us his servants. They have honored it not only by this interest and respect, but also by other kinds no less than this. Imperial letters are despatched with instructions for prisoners to have their bonds undone: just as our Lord was in Hades and released all those held by death, so too the servants contribute what they can in imitation of the Lord's kindness by undoing the material bonds, since they are powerless over the spiritual ones. [6]

We also honor this week. I too went out with you extending a word of instruction in place of palms, depositing the two mites like the widow. [7] Then those with palm branches went out, crying aloud in the words, "Hosanna in the highest! Blessed is he who comes in the name of the Lord." [8] Let us too go out, give evidence of a vigorous purpose in place of the palm branches, and cry aloud, just as we sang today's response, *Praise the Lord, O my soul, I shall praise the Lord all my life* (vv.1-2). [9] The second verse is also David's like the first – or, rather, neither second nor first is David's, both stemming from the Spirit's grace: while the inspired author uttered it, it was the Paraclete who moved the author's tongue. [10] Hence his saying, "My tongue the pen of a fluent scribe:" just as the pen writes not of itself but with the direction of the one using it, so too the tongue of the inspired authors gave voice not of itself but by the grace of God. But why he did not say simply, "My tongue the pen of a scribe" instead of "pen of a (524) fluent scribe?" For you to learn that wisdom is spiritual – hence its great ease and swift movement. Human beings in giving voice on their own account, you see, require much time in composing, planning and pausing, whereas in that other case, since the words flowed as from a spring and there was no obstacle, and instead the flood of ideas surpassed the movement of the tongue, he therefore said, "My tongue the pen of a fluent scribe." The ideas bubbled up from below in great abundance, he is saying – hence the great fluency. There is no need of pondering, nor of attention and labor. [11]

Let us, however, see what he is saying. *Praise the Lord, my soul.* Let us also sing this together with David: if he is not present in body, at least he is in spirit. For proof that the righteous are present with us, and sing along with us, listen to what Abraham says to the rich man: when he said, "Send Lazarus so that my brothers may learn what happens in Hades and put their affairs in order," he replied to him, "They have Moses and the prophets." [12] Actually, Moses and all the prophets were long dead in the body, but in their writings they had them. After all, if a person sets up a lifeless image of son or dear one and thinks that person, though dead, is present, and through the lifeless image he imagines him, much more do we enjoy the communion of the saints through the divine Scriptures, having in them images not of their bodies but of their souls, the words spoken by them being images of their very souls. [13]

Are you interested in learning that the righteous are also

present to the living? No one calls the dead as witnesses; but Christ called them to witness to his own divinity, and before them David himself, to convince you that he is alive: when the Jews had doubts about him, he said to them, "What do you think of the Christ? whose son is he? They replied to him, David's. He said to them, How, then, does David by the Spirit call him Lord in the words, The Lord said to my lord, sit at my right hand?" [14] Do you see how David is alive? After all, if he were not alive, he would not have called him to witness to his divinity. He did not say, How, then, did David by the Spirit call him Lord, but "does call him Lord?" so as to bring out that he is still present and speaks through his writings.

Of old David sang in psalms, as today we do along with David. He had a harp with lifeless strings; the Church has a harp strung with living strings. Our tongues are strings of the harp which, while giving voice to different sounds, produce a devotion that is harmonious: men and women, old and young differ in age, but do not differ in respect of melody, the Spirit modulating each one's voice and producing the one note in every singer. [15] It is just as David himself declared in summoning every age and each nature to this symphony in the words, "Let every breath praise the Lord. Praise the Lord, my soul!" [16] (522) Why did he omit the flesh? why did he not address the body? surely he did not divide the living being in two? Not at all; rather, he summoned the artist first. For proof that he did not separate the flesh from the spirit, listen to what he says elsewhere: "O God, my God, for you I watch at dawn. My soul thirsted for you; how often my flesh longs for you on earth." [17] But show me the flesh itself summoned in hymns, someone may say. "Bless the Lord, my soul, and everything within me his holy name." [18] Do you see the flesh also sharing in the symphony?

What is the meaning of "and everything within me his holy name"? Nerves, bones, veins, arteries and all the organs within. How can what is within praise God? It has no voice, no mouth, no tongue. The soul can – but how can what is within praise God, having no voice, no tongue, no mouth? In the way "the heavens recount the glory of God:" [19] just as the heavens have no tongue, no mouth, no lips, but strike the onlookers with the beauty of the sight and commission them in wonderment to praise of their maker, so too what is within us; if you address your mind to it, if you note the differences in quality, in action, in power, in harmony, in formation, in position, in number, you will give vent to that inspired utterance, "How your works are magnified, O Lord! You made everything in wisdom." [20] Do you see how the entrails bless God without voice or mouth or tongue? So why does he address the soul? Lest it be distracted when the tongue is giving utterance, which we often experience in praying and hymn-singing, and to ensure that the symphony occurs with all participating: when you pray without listening to the words of God, how will God listen to your petition?

When, then, you say, *Praise the Lord, my soul*, it means, Let your petitions be lifted up within from the bottom of your heart. Paul also says, remember, "I shall pray with the spirit, but I shall also pray with my mind." [21] The soul is an excellent musician, it is an artist; the body is an instrument, filling the role of harp and flute and lyre. Some musicians, therefore, do not always perform with all the instruments, but at times they make use of them and at other times they lay them aside, the time not always being available to them for music, and hence they do not employ the instruments constantly. God, however, wished to teach you that you ought always sing praise to him and bless him, and so he joined the instrument to the artist permanently. For proof, in fact, that we ought always be praising, listen to what the apostle says, "Pray without interruption, in everything give thanks." [22] So since we ought pray without interruption, without interruption the instrument accompanies the musician. *Praise the Lord, my soul*. Formerly David said this with a single tongue, but now that he is dead, he utters it with countless tongues, not only ours but also those everywhere throughout the world. Do you see that he is not dead but alive? How could the one who has so many tongues and gives voice through so many mouths be dead? Praise is a really wonderful thing: it purifies our soul and instils in it deep piety.

Do you want to learn the efficacy of hymns sung to God? (523) By singing hymns the three young men extinguished the furnace of Babylon – or, rather, instead of extinguishing it, they did what was more remarkable, trampling with their feet on the burning fire as though on mud. [23] Hymn-singing of this kind entered the prison in Paul's case and loosed his bonds, opened the doors of the prison, shook the foundations and frightened the jailer with deep shock, the text saying that Paul and Silas were singing hymns at midnight. [24] Then what happened? What? Something completely novel and unexpected: bonds were loosened, the bound man tied up the one at liberty. It is the nature of bonds to hold the bound person quite securely and keep them subject, whereas in this case the jailer, who was at liberty, fell at the feet of Paul, who was bound. It is, in fact, the nature of material bonds to hold fast the bound person, whereas such is the force of the bonds in Christ as to make those at liberty subject to the bound. He cast them into the interior prison, and when they were inside they opened the doors outside. He secured their feet to the stocks, and their feet thus secured loosened the hands of others.

Then the jailer fell down before him, the text says, in fear and trembling, groaning, anguished and in tears. What happened then? were you not bound? were you not held securely? Why are you surprised, mortal that you are, if he opened the prison when he actually had the power to open the heavens as well? "Whatever you bind on earth will be bound in heaven, and whatever you loose on earth will be loosed on heaven." [25] He loosed the bonds of sin: why are you surprised if he looses bonds of iron? He loosed the bonds of demons, freed souls bound by them: why are you surprised if he undoes the chains of the bound? Note the double marvel: he loosed and bound in turn, loosening their bonds and binding their heart. They did not realise, you see, that they were loosed. He opened and closed: he opened the doors of the prison, and he closed the eyes of the heart of those bound in case they should notice the opened doors, in case they should also take advantage of their release to take to flight. Do you see binder and looser, opener and closer?

It happened at night for this reason, that the event might occur without causing alarm and be free of all disturbance; the apostles did nothing to gain notoriety and publicity. The chief jailer fell down before him. So what did Paul do? Do you see his miracle? do you see his astonishing deeds? Notice also his care, notice also his kindness. "He cried out in the words, Do yourself no harm: we are all in here." [26] He did not allow the one who put them in harsh bonds to meet a harsh death, he carried no grudge: "We are all in here," he said. Paul included himself amongst the prisoners. On seeing what had happened, the other man marveled, was astonished at the miracle and gave thanks to God. The jailer proved truly worthy of deep care and kindness, not believing the events to be trickery. Why did he not believe the events to be trickery? He heard them singing praise to God: a trickster never sings praise to God. He had admitted many tricksters, since he was a jailer; but none of them had ever shown signs of such a feat, had not loosed bonds, had not given evidence of such care. (524) Paul, in fact, had elected to be bound and not to flee so as to free him from death; he came rushing in with sword and lamp in hand, the devil wanting to snatch him from repentance by suicide, but in a loud voice Paul more swiftly gained the salvation of his soul. In fact, he did not simply cry out, but said in a loud voice, "We are all in here." The jailer marveled at his solicitude, the free man fell down before the bound man – and what does he say? "Sirs, what must I do to be saved?"[27] It was you who did the binding, and are you at a loss? it was you who secured them to the stocks, and are you searching for a way to repentance and salvation?

Do you see the ardor? do you see the zeal? Far from delaying, though he was released from fear, he was not released from doing good, but at once took steps to secure the salvation of his own soul. It was night – midnight, in fact. He did not say, Let us think about it, let day dawn; instead, he immediately made for salvation. This man is a wonderful person, he says, he surpasses human nature. He saw his wonderworking, he marveled at his kindness. Though suffering countless abuses at my hands and being at death's door, he took me, bound as I was, into his hands, and though in a position to dispose of me, he not only did nothing of the sort but even prevented me, when on the point of killing myself, from cutting my throat. He was right to say, "Sirs, what must I do to be saved?" I mean, in the case of the apostles, it was not simply the miracles that won the believers over, but their life ahead of the miracles. Hence Scripture says, "Let your light shine in people's sight so that they may see your good works and glorify your father in heaven."[28]

Did you see the jailer's ardor? Notice also Paul's ardor. he did not put him off, he did not scorn him; instead, though being in bonds, though being in the stocks, the victim of scourging, he immediately began his initiation, and with him all his household, and after the spiritual washing and after the spiritual banquet he laid before him also a material one.[29] But why did he shake the prison? He wanted to prompt the jailer to an insight into what was happening; he loosed the material bonds of the prisoners so as to loose the spiritual bonds of the jailer. Christ did the opposite to this. A paralytic approached him with a double paralysis, of sin and of body. [30] First he released the paralysis of sin in these words, "Child, your sins are forgiven." Then, when they doubted and blasphemed and said, "No one can forgive sins except God alone," he wanted to show them that he is truly God, he wanted them to make the judgement from their own mouths so that he would be in a position to say, I judge you from your own mouths, You said no one can forgive sins except God alone; lo, I forgive sins, confess my divinity, from your own judgement I deliver the verdict. In the one case, however, the spiritual comes first, and the physical later, whereas in this case it is the opposite, first the material bonds are removed and then the spiritual.

Do you see the efficacy of hymns? the force of praise? the force of prayer? The efficacy of prayer, then, is always great; (525) but prayer with fasting renders the soul stronger: then it is that we enjoy deep sobriety of thought, then the mind is aroused and the soul fixes its gaze on all that is above. This is the reason Scripture always associated prayer with fasting. How and when? "Do not deprive each other except by agreement for the sake of devoting yourselves to fasting and prayer," and again in another place, "This kind does not leave except by prayer and fasting," and again in another place, "After praying and fasting they laid hands on them." [31] Do you see prayer occurring everywhere along with fasting? Then it is, you see, that music is performed on the lyre more sweetly and properly. The chords are not moist, loosened with the intoxication of greed; instead, thinking is taut, the mind alert, the soul awake. I mean, if when we have something urgent to say to our friends, we take them aside and then converse, much more is it necessary to do this with God, going into an inner chamber with deep tranquillity; and we shall attain absolutely everything for which we were suitably making our petition.

Prayer, in fact, is a great good when it happens with a mind thankful and alert.[32] How will it be thankful? If we train ourselves to give thanks to God not only when we receive our requests but also when we miss out. God, you see, sometimes grants our requests, sometimes does not; but in both cases he acts for our good so that whether you gain your request or not, you gain in not gaining. There are times, in fact, when it is more to our advantage not to receive what we ask than to receive it: if it were not to our advantage in many cases not to receive, he would always grant our requests without fail; but missing out to our advantage is to gain. Hence he also delays our request on many occasions, not wanting to put us off, but skilfully arranging for continued supplication by the delay in giving. You see, often when we receive what we ask, on receipt we slacken our zeal for prayer, and so in his wish to promote our devotion to supplication he delays his consent. Fond parents also behave this way: children's indolence and recourse to childish games they keep in check by the promise of a very big present; hence sometimes they put it off, sometimes they award it. There are times, in fact, when what we ask for is harmful; but God, who knows better what is good for us, does not accede to our requests, making arrangements for our good even when we are not aware of it.

What is remarkable in our not being heard when this happened even in Paul's case? Often, in fact, he failed to get what he asked for; and not only did he not get upset, but he even thanked God. "For this I thrice besought the Lord," the word "thrice" suggesting many times. Now, if Paul asked many times without success, how much more should we therefore persist. Let us observe, however, when he did not receive what he many times asked for, how he felt about not receiving. In fact, he did not only not get upset, but he even boasted (526) when he did not receive: after saying, "For this I thrice besought the Lord, and he replied to me, My grace is

sufficient for you, for my power is made perfect in infirmity,"
he went on, "So I shall be very glad to boast of my
infirmities." [33] Do you see a grateful servant? He begged to
be rid of the infirmity, and God did not accede; Paul did not
only not get upset, but even boasts of the infirmity.

Let this be the way we also conduct our prayers: whether
God grants or does not grant our requests, let us thank God
for both, since he does both for our good. If it is within his
power to give, it is therefore in his power also when to give,
what to give, and not to give. You do not know what is for
your good as he knows. Often you ask for what is harmful
and damaging; he on the other hand, out of care of your
salvation, attends not to the request but considers in every
case before that what is for your good. After all, if parents
according to the flesh do not provide their children with
everything they ask for, not because they have no regard for
them but because they take special care of them, much more
does God do it, being more loving and knowing also more
than anyone what is for our good.

Let us therefore devote ourselves constantly to prayer, not
only by day but also by night. Listen, in fact, to what the
inspired author himself says, "I would rise at midnight to
praise you for the judgements of your righteousness." [34]
Though a royal personage with so many responsibilities,
entrusted with populace and cities and rule of nations, taking
measures for peace, suppressing war, seeing an indescribable
weight of affairs ever pressing upon him, with not the
slightest possibility of resting, he devotes himself to prayer
not only by day but also by night. Now, if the king living in
such luxury, with such responsibilities, enveloped in such
affairs, does not rest even at night, and instead perseveres in
saying prayers more carefully than the monks situated in
the mountains, what excuse shall we have, tell me, living as
we do at such leisure, opting for a private life free of public
involvement, for not only sleeping all night but not

performing the prescribed prayers with due vigilance even in the daytime? [35]

Prayer is a great weapon, prayer is a wonderful adornment, security and haven, a treasury of good things, wealth beyond threat. When we make requests of human beings, we need an outlay of money, servile flattery, much to-ing and fro-ing and negotiating. Often, in fact, it is not possible to make a direct approach to their lordships personally to grant a favor: it is necessary first to wait upon their ministers or managers or administrators with money and words and every other means, and only then through them to be in a position to receive the request. With God, on the contrary, it is not like this: it not so much on the recommendation of others as on our own request that he grants the favor. In this case, too, both the one receiving it and the one not receiving it are better off, whereas in the case of human beings we often come off worse in both cases.

Since, then, for those approaching God the gain is greater and the facility greater, do not neglect prayer: it is then in particular that he will be reconciled with you when you on your own account appeal to him, when (527) you present a mind purified, thoughts that are alert, when you do not make idle petitions, as many people do, their tongue saying the words while their soul wanders in every direction[36] – through the house, the marketplace, the city streets. It is all the devil's doing: since he knows that at that time we are able to attain forgiveness of sins, he wants to block the haven of prayer to us, and at that time he goes on the attack to distract us from the sense of the words so that we may depart the worse rather than the better for it.

Aware of this, therefore, mortal that you are, when you approach God, consider who it is you approach: the trustworthiness of the one about to grant you the favor is sufficient to summon you to vigilance. Set your gaze on heaven, and ponder who it is to whom your words are directed. After all, if you are talking with a human being somewhat elevated in human ranking, no matter if you are the most careless person of all, you put yourself completely on your mettle and bid your soul to be alert. Much more, then, if we give thought to the fact that we are speaking with the Lord of the angels, shall we find sufficient grounds for paying attention. If, however, there is need to specify some other means (528) for us to avoid this indifference, [37] this is what I would say. Often we perform the prayer and take our leave without hearing anything of what we have said. Should we realise this, therefore, let us immediately repeat it; if the same thing should happen to us again, let us recite it a third and fourth time, and not desist from praying before we recite it completely with mind alert. [38] If the devil notices that we do not give up until we recite it with enthusiasm and an alert mind, he will then give up ambushing us in the knowledge that he will achieve nothing more from his scheming than often forcing us to repeat the same prayer.

We incur many wounds each day, dearly beloved, from people at home and abroad, in the marketplace, at home, from business public and private, from neighbors, from friends. Let us apply remedies to these wounds at the time of prayer. [39] God is able, you see, if we approach him with mind alert, soul aflame and conscience eager, and we beg his pardon, to grant us forgiveness for all the failings. May it be the good fortune of us all to attain this, thanks to the grace and lovingkindness of our Lord Jesus Christ, to whom with the Father and the Holy Spirit be the glory for ages of ages. Amen.

Select Bibliography

Aubineau, M., "Restitution de quatorze folios du codex hierosolymitain, Photios 47, au codex Saint-Sabas 32. Prédications de Chrysostome à Constantinople et notamment à Saint-Irène," *JThS* 43 (1992) 528-44

Barthélemy, D., *Les Devanciers d'Aquila*, VTS X, Leiden, 1963

Baur, P. C., *John Chrysostom and his Time*, 2 vols, Eng. trans., London-Glasgow, 1959,1960

Bouyer, L., *The Spirituality of the New Testament and the Fathers*, Eng. trans., London, 1963

Drewery, B., "Antiochien," *TRE* 3, 103-113

Fernandez Marcos, N., "Some reflections on the Antiochian text of the Septuagint," in D. Fraenkel et al (edd.), *Studien zur Septuaginta – Robert Hanhart zu Ehren*, Göttingen, 1990, 219-229

_____ , "The Lucianic text in the Books of Kingdoms," in A. Pietersma et al (edd.), *De Septuaginta*, Mississauga, 1984

_____ , *The Septuagint in Context: Introduction to the Greek Versions of the Bible*, Eng. trans., Boston-Leiden, 2001

Hill, R. C., "St. John Chrysostom's teaching on inspiration in 'Six Homilies on Isaiah'," *VC* 22 (1968) 19-37

_____ ,"*Akribeia*: a principle of Chrysostom's exegesis," *Colloquium* 14 (Oct. 1981) 32-36

_____ , "Chrysostom's terminology for the inspired Word," *EstBíb* 41 1983) 367-73

_____ , *St. John Chrysostom's Homilies on Genesis*, FOTC 74,82,87, 1986, 1990, 1992

_____ , "Psalm 45: a *locus classicus* for patristic thinking on biblical inspiration," *StudP* 25 (1991) 95-100

_____ , "Chrysostom's Commentary on the Psalms: homilies or tracts?" in P. Allen et al (edd.), *Prayer and Spirituality in the Early Church* I, Brisbane 1998

_____ , "A pelagian commentator on the Psalms?" *ITQ* 65 (1998) 263-71

_____, *St. John Chrysostom. Commentary on the Psalms*, 2 vols, Brookline MA, 1998

_____, "Chrysostom's homilies on David and Saul," *SVTQ* 44 (2000) 123-41

_____, "St. John Chrysostom's homilies on Hannah," *SVTQ* 45 (2001) 319-38

_____, "St. John Chrysostom's Six Homilies on Isaiah 6," *SVTQ*

_____, "Chrysostom on the obscurity of the Old Testament," *OCP* 67 (2001) 371-83

_____, "Psalm 42, a classic text for Antiochene spirituality," *ITQ*

Kelly, J. N. D., *Early Christian Doctrines*, 5th ed., New York, 1978

_____, *Golden Mouth. The Story of John Chrysostom. Ascetic, Preacher, Bishop*, Ithaca NY, 1995

Leroux, J.-M., "Johannes Chrysostomus," *TRE* 17, 118-27

Mayer, W., Allen, P., *John Chrysostom*, The Early Church Fathers, London-New York, 2000

Schäublin, C., "Diodor von Tarsus," *TRE* 8, 763-67

_____, *Untersuchungen zu Methode und Herkunft der Antiochenischen Exegese*, Theophaneia: Beiträge zur Religions- und Kirchengeschichte des Altertums 23, Köln-Bonn, 1974

Ternant, P., "La θεωρία d'Antioche dans le cadre de sens de l''Ecriture," *Bib* 34 (1953) 135-58,354-383,456-86

Vaccari, A., "La θεωρία nella scuola esegetica di Antiochia," *Bib* 1 (1920) 3-36

Wallace-Hadrill, D. S., *Christian Antioch. A Study of Early Christian Thought in the East*, Cambridge, 1982

Young, F., *Biblical Exegesis and the Formation of Christian Culture*, Cambridge, 1997

Zincone, S., "Le omelie di Giovanni Crisostomo 'De prophetiarum obscuritate'," *StudP* 32 (1997) 393-409

_____, *Giovanni Crisostomo. Omelie sull'oscurità delle profezie*, Verba Seniorum N.S. 12, Roma, 1998

NOTES

Notes to Chrysostom's Homilies
On the Obscurity of the Old Testament

Notes to Homily One

[1] The text of the homilies was edited in the eighteenth century by Bernard de Montfaucon, and appears in PG 56.163-92 (nos. retained in above text for convenience); the modern critical edition is by Sergio Zincone, *Omelie sull'oscurità delle profezie*, in which differences from the PG text are noted (56-58). For a detailed study, see also my article, "Chrysostom on the obscurity of the Old Testament." Is there a particular Isaian text on which the homilies are a commentary? In opening the final homily on Isa 6, Chrysostom speaks of the series as a journey across the ocean of the text that he is about to conclude: does that series follow these two? For the terms used of Old and New Testament composition and composers, see my article, "Chrysostom's terminology for the inspired Word."

[2] Chrysostom does not speak so much of readers of the Word (though he consistently uses the conventional term Γραφή, suggesting written text) as listeners, his congregation accessing it through liturgical proclamation and homilies on it.

[3] Heb 5.11.

[4] The notion of ἀσθένεια, the limitations of the human condition, is an element in Chrysostom's theology of the biblical Word, in which by an act of considerateness, συγκατάβασις, God communicates to us in human language (just as he does in the humanity of the Word enfleshed in Jesus). "Weakness" does not do justice to the notion. In the case of this homily, the particular limitation in question is the obduracy of Old Testament Jews.

[5] One wonders if Chrysostom's congregations appreciated this approach to their infirmity, and might not have settled for brevity in place of length and profusion, even Paul having admitted that length could be a problem.

[6] Cf Heb 7.2-3.

[7] Isa 53.8 LXX – hardly the Isaian text referred to at the outset. Chrysostom, of course, is suspicious of a kataphatic approach to Christology that recklessly looks for comprehension of the incomprehensible.

[8] Phrases like this occurring in Chrysostom and Theodoret give grounds for doubting their full commitment to the *communicatio idiomatum*.

[9] Montfaucon admits that his predecessor Savile preferred the verb here in the active, "he generated him." Zincone disagrees.

[10] This is the preferred approach of apophatic theologians like

Chrysostom, who would rather cite the positive statement of Scripture than engage in speculative argument.

¹¹ John 3.12.

¹² It has been a lengthy Christological digression in a homily devoted to the Old Testament. Montfaucon rejects the view that this mention of a treatment of Melchizedek fixes the date at 387, when one of the Homilies (the seventh) against the Jews was given in which Melchizedek figures.

¹³ The relative clarity of the New Testament and obscurity of the Old are due to two factors, Chrysostom holds, one essential, one accidental: content and circumstance. Doctrines are clearer in the New, obfuscation has been deliberately added to the Old by the authors for fear of reprisals.

¹⁴ Who are those present who are not friends, but who may become friends on hearing the preacher's explanation? Is there a likelihood that Jews would be present and be convinced by his unsympathetic depiction of them? See notes 23 and 41.

¹⁵ The proverbial rationale for the Jews' continuing misfortunes: their treatment of Jesus.

¹⁶ 1 Kgs 19.10.

¹⁷ Matt 23.37.

¹⁸ Isa 1.15.

¹⁹ A loose conflation of Luke 11.47 and Matt 23.31-32.

²⁰ Jer 38.4. Though Chrysostom claims to be illustrating the inherent obscurity, ἀσάφεια, of the Old Testament, his theme would basically seem to be the obduracy of the Jews. Of course, he is not alone among the Fathers in developing this thesis about the Jews and their contemporary misfortunes, "They got what they deserved."

Chrysostom's reference to the invaders as Persians led some early commentators to sense lack of authenticity in the homily; but Montfaucon rightly claims such imprecision occurs elsewhere in his works (he might have cited commentary on Ps 4.3, e.g.), and Zincone concurs.

²¹ Cf Acts 6.11,14. "Our dignity and their reprobation" is what the Fathers were out to establish in their reading of the Old Testament. Cf note 33.

²² A conflation of Matt 26.61 and John 2.19.

²³ A precis of Acts 21.20-21. Chrysostom, probably because of the presence of "unfriendly" listeners in the congregation, is constantly having to document his points from the text of Scripture.

²⁴ Jer 36.1-2. This "promise," to develop his thesis from textual evidence, Chrysostom keeps harking back to.

²⁵ Jer 36.3. Yes, as we observed in note 20, this is the line Chrysostom should be pursuing, not simply the obduracy of the Jews.

²⁶ Yet again Chrysostom is trying (despite himself) to convince his listeners that he really is on the point, and is sticking to the evidence of the text.

²⁷ This and later verses are so far from the wording of any known form of Jer 36.4 that (*pace* Montfaucon) they may simply be Chrysostom's

paraphrase of the next development rather than quotation of, say, a local form of the LXX.

²⁸ Jer 36.5.

²⁹ Chrysostom continues to dispense snatches of the text without keeping to the strict sequence of events or word order.

³⁰ Montfaucon notes that the manuscripts make no mention of November (cf Jer 36.22), and Zincone does not include it. Referring to the Macedonian calendar in use in Antioch (cf also its use in 2 Macc 11), Chrysostom is anxious to relate the incident to winter, which would not be the case if the "ninth month" was numbered from Dios (November) and not from Xanthicus (April) in that calendar. We should be precise about this dating, he is saying, as Scripture is precise in relating the destruction of the scroll to the fire and the wintry conditions. It is axiomatic for Antiochenes that "nothing is passed over by the divine Scripture" (and should not be by the commentator).

³¹ Jer 36.23, still loosely quoted. Again the "promise" to establish the thesis from the text.

³² Cf Jer 36.26.

³³ Rom 10.20, citing Isa 65.1, which Chrysostom continues beyond Paul's citation – typical of his (more than usually) loose recall of scriptural loci in this homily. Again there is the concern to account for "our blessings and their troubles," "the dignity and glory coming to the nations and the dishonor awaiting (the Jews);" cf note 21.

³⁴ Chrysostom is continuing to sustain his double thesis, the obduracy of the Jews and the need for oblique statement in the Scriptures.

³⁵ Acts 9.15; 2 Cor 11.2. There is a shift in the argument at this point: the obscurity of the Old Testament, if intentional, is only partial.

³⁶ The reading of this clause is debated. As an Antiochene Chrysostom does not generally dwell on two levels of meaning in Old Testament texts; but he is prepared to recognize an eschatological sense in some texts, especially with New Testament encouragement.

³⁷ 2 Cor 3.12-14. Paul in these chapters seems uncertain as to whether the veil covered Moses' face, the Jews' face, or the Law; and Chrysostom also oscillates.

³⁸ Exod 34.33-35.

³⁹ Even if eloquent on its deficiencies, Chrysostom, if less insistently than his fellow Antiochene Theodoret, maintains the continuing value of the Law against Marcion and others who would deny it – a rather particular application of his general thesis of the obscurity of the Old Testament. Paul's argument in 2 Cor 3-4, which Chrysostom would like to be invoking, accentuates rather the obsolescence of the once splendid gift, not its partial verity, as here.

⁴⁰ This is perhaps a slight shift in position on the reason for the Law's obscurity, suggesting lack of faith rather than obduracy or risk to authors and their material.

⁴¹ Is it of Jews in the congregation that Chrysostom speaks in regard to

the Law's role as "your" guide? If not, then he is maintaining a role for the Law in the formation of Christians.

⁴² The phrase, "the kinship of the Law with grace," implies also the relationship of all the Old Testament to the New.

Notes to Homily Two

¹ Chrysostom can cajole or expostulate when confronting his congregations, the latter particularly if attendance has suffered. In this case he takes to cajoling them, perhaps because of the abstruse nature of the subject already treated of once, no particular biblical text seeming to be in focus for the day, such as a liturgical reading. The congregation's response, ὑπακοή, which in some cases can be a sung responsorium, is at least attentiveness (the rendering of Fronto de Duc, "obedientia," as in the homily on Isa 45.6-7 above, again seems wide of the mark; see note 31 below). Such attentiveness can be elicited by a pleasing array of figures for the ministry of the Word and by flattery of the congregation's wild enthusiasm.

² In the former homily (delivered πρώην, "the other day" or "the day before yesterday") Chrysostom promised to convince his listeners, who included some who were "unfriendly" (possibly Jews?), of the truth of his thesis, and did so by consistently documenting it; see notes there 14,23,26,31,41.

³ 2 Cor 3.14, from the passage dwelt on in the latter stages of the former homily.

⁴ See note 4 in the former homily.

⁵ As note 13 in the former homily observes, Chrysostom seems to say there that one factor in the greater clarity of the New Testament is its content, certain doctrines being included that are not in the Old Testament. Here, on the contrary, he says the τέλεια διδάγματα of the New Testament were in fact stored in the Old, though hidden by veil later removed for us. This position is closer to Augustine's, of course, *in Vetere Novum latet, in Novo Vetus patet.*

The motive for the obscurity was a kindly one, God's onsiderateness, συγκατάβασις (the verb form in use here), for the Jews' limitations (see note 4) – a favorite notion of Chrysostom's, of course.

⁶ The term employed, προφητεία, as the introduction observes, applies to all Old Testament composition (at an oral level primarily, as is suggested in what follows), without denying inspiration to New Testament works – and in fact Chrysostom proceeds to cite a New Testament example. Such inspired composition includes prophecy.

⁷ John 2.18-19,21.

⁸ John 2.22.

⁹ John 15.22.

¹⁰ Chrysostom now adduces a third reason for the obscurity of the Old Testament in addition to the two identified in the former homily (see note 13 there), contents and accidental obfuscation applied by the authors –

namely, the fact that language of the version currently in use (by both Jews and Christians) differs from the original.

[11] Again the implication that for most people the Bible is encountered through public (liturgical or paraliturgical) reading. For many in the churches of Antioch, of course, neither Hebrew nor Greek was their native tongue, Syriac being Theodoret's, for example.

[12] Chrysostom does not claim to be among these polylingual savants nor even to know Hebrew; in his (early?) Psalms Commentary, whenever he essays some comment on the original Hebrew, he often comes to grief, whereas in commenting on Genesis (with greater maturity?) he is prepared to speak of "those who know that language" and imply his ignorance of it.

[13] Unlike Theodoret, Chrysostom does not adopt the legendary account in the Letter of Aristeas of this translation by the Seventy (LXX), simply accepting its being carried out for practical reasons. We would like to have heard him say something on the later development of his own local form of this Greek version.

[14] As Chrysostom and Theodoret speak of the Old Testament as προφητικός for reasons outlined above, so the New Testament generally is ἀποστολικός. The role of the former in guiding us to Christ upholds its status.

[15] Ps 2.8.

[16] Isa 53.7 LXX; 11.10,9.

[17] Pss 47.5; 110.1.

[18] In addition to Paul's address to the Areopagus adopting a philosophical approach in Acts 17, Chrysostom is thinking of an address like that to the Jews in the synagogue of Pisidian Antioch in Acts 13 that rests on the biblical background to Jesus.

[19] Has Chrysostom exhausted his treatment of the obscurity of the Old Testament? He now launches into a speculative discussion of the origin of languages, at best marginally relevant to that topic. Not having the equipment of the φιλόλογοι of whom he spoke in the homily on Isaiah 45.6-7 (see note 33 there), he can only approach the question from a moral point of view.

[20] To build up the case of the person who objects to God capriciously imposing diversity of language as a penalty for sin, Chrysostom underplays – but implicitly accepts – the Fall in a deliberate misrepresentation of Gen 3 (the Babel account in ch. 11 being suppressed for the time being).

[21] As in his Commentary on Genesis, indifference, ῥαθυμία, is identified as the sin of the first parents.

[22] Not only the obscurity of the Old Testament but even the ensuing discussion of diversity of languages have dropped from sight as the speaker embarks on an exposition of the sequel to the Fall.

[23] Luke 23.43 – a little bit of sophistry here, with a mere play upon words in place of solid argument.

²⁴ Though Chrysostom realises he has strayed from the topic, he now focuses on security, ἀσφάλεια, whereas the original topic was rather obscurity, ἀσάφεια.

²⁵ The figure of the debt he promised to discharge has been in the speaker's thoughts from the former homily; but these were not the items relevant to his theme, which has to do rather with the obscurity of the Old Testament generally than simply its language. He seems also to imply that he will return to the theme on even another occasion and deal with unfinished business, whereas we have but the two homilies on it.

²⁶ Rom 15.30-31; Eph 6.19.

²⁷ 2 Cor 1.10-11, with some individual textual features.

²⁸ A good case is being made for communal prayer in synaxeis presided over by the clergy; but we have to question its relevance to the obscurity of the Old Testament.

²⁹ Acts 12.5. The example of Peter follows that of Paul, and (as before) that is the order in which they come to Chrysostom's lips.

³⁰ Montfaucon suggests the text is corrupt at this point. He also sees this datum about public prayer for the bishop as one of the features of the homilies, and to Zincone it shows (conclusively?) that Chrysostom is not yet a bishop himself. We learn also of differing church practice for the initiated and the uninitiated.

³¹ Again the use of ὑπακούειν for the congregation's concerted response (sometimes in song), not merely obedience or concurrence (see note 1).

³² Gen 11.1.

³³ 1 Cor 2.14.

³⁴ The exegesis of the Genesis text, with its simple play upon words and neglect of the wider context – in defiance of the principles Chrysostom himself outlined in his homily on Jer 10.23 – reminds one of rabbinic commentary.

³⁵ Gen 3.19.

³⁶ Gen 1.26; 9.2.

³⁷ Mal 4.5-6, of doubtful relevance to the argument, let alone the original topic, now well out of sight.

³⁸ Isa 11.5.

³⁹ Isa 11.4.

⁴⁰ Chrysostom probably has Sir 29.20 in mind, though his classical education would have made him familiar with the more celebrated Delphic and Socratic dictum, Know yourself. The treatment now is thoroughly moral, general considerations of the Old Testament's obscurity being well out of sight.

⁴¹ Gen 18.27.

⁴² Sir 10.9.

⁴³ Editors of modern versions make exactly the same comment on the Greek text of this verse.

⁴⁴ An Antiochene would hasten to resist any suggestion of a dualistic depreciation of the human condition.

[45] Isa 14.13.

[46] Cf Isa 40.6. Chrysostom always warms to the theme of the futility of the vulgar display of the high and mighty.

[47] Chrysostom has gained a reputation for misogynism from passages like this; but it is perhaps simply a consequence of his congregation being (principally or exclusively) male, a mixed congregation suggesting a different example.

[48] Sir 17.31. The original topic now well behind him, the preacher is off into a lesson on theodicy, with some questionable astronomy called into service.

[49] There are numerous other places where Chrysostom defines the purpose of Scripture as moral and hagiographical; certainly he often shows little appreciation of a biblical author's dogmatic purpose, like the Deuteronomist's, as we saw in connection with the homilies on Hannah and on David and Saul. In this text, where he defines his own role as homilist (by analogy with a trainer preparing wrestlers for combat), we see also the process of transmission of the scriptural Word in the early Church: the preacher does the reading and explaining for the benefit of the congregation, this twofold task not falling within their competence – though Chrysostom can be quoted elsewhere for recommending them to take the Bible in hand in the family circle for private reading.

[50] Pss 140.3; 57.4. As the Antiochenes with their eastern reverence for divine transcendence, on the one hand, and their incarnational thinking on the other had to balance the roles of divine grace and human effort in the process of salvation, so in the Scriptures they had to recognize the συγκατάβασις by which the divine is communicated in figurative terms without infringing either divine transcendence or human dignity. Some groups failed to respect this balance, Chrysostom is saying.

[51] Cf Ps 12.2, cited in a form slightly different from its occurrence in Chrysostom's Psalms Commentary.

[52] Ps 5.9.

[53] Instead of being content with an illustration that bears (remotely) on the original topic, the speaker takes the bait of its moral content to digress again.

[54] Isa 43.26. Textual readings in parts of this moral digression vary between the critic, κατήγορος, and the abuser, κακήγορος.

[55] Prov 18.17 LXX.

[56] 1 Tim 1.12-13,15; 1 Cor 15.9.

[57] 1 Cor 4.5.

[58] Cf 1 Cor 2.11.

[59] Cf Matt 23.27.

[60] For Chrysostom's church, of course, baptism was the principal sacrament of reconciliation, there being no other separate rite. But unlike the Novatian rigorists his church allowed the possibility of forgiveness of sins committed after baptism – for instance, by the self-abasement (ἐξομολό γησις) of public sinners he describes in the third homily on David and Saul.

[61] Luke 5.8. This Petrine example Montfaucon, on the basis of one ms, has inserted into the text, both of them encouraged by its appearance in the homily on the devil as tempter delivered shortly afterwards, where Chrysostom claims to have cited Peter as well amongst the self-critics listed in our homily. See introduction above.

[62] Cf Matt 10.3.

[63] Luke 18.13,11.

[64] Gal 6.4.

[65] Ps 38.4.

[66] Isa 6.5.

[67] Dan 3.29 Grk.

[68] Exod 23.1.

[69] Ps 100.5.

[70] Matt 12.37. Is Chrysostom speaking of those who encourage calumny by listening to it, or of those who are the object of calumny? He appears to use ἀκούειν in both senses.

[71] Cf Matt 18.6.

[72] Matt 18.15.

Notes to Chrysostom's Homilies on the Psalms

[1] We are not well-acquainted with byzantine lectionaries in use in Chrysostom's churches, according to M. Aubineau, "*Restitution de quatorze folios du codex hierosolymitain, Photios 47, au codex Saint-Sabas 32. Prédications de Chrysostome à Constantinople et notamment à Sainte-Irène,*" 537.

[2] Cf Eph 5.9; Col 3.16.

[3] Cf M.-J. Rondeau, *Les commentaires patristiques du Psautier (IIIe-Ve siècles),* I *Les travaux des pères grecs et latins sur le Psautier,* II *Exégèse prosopologique et théologie* (Orientalia Christiana Analecta 219, 220), Roma, 1982, 1985.

[4] *Ep.* 112,20 (PL 22.928-29).

[5] Cf my English translation, *St. John Chrysostom. Commentary on the Psalms.*

[6] Cf the reconstitued text by R. Devreesse, *Le commentaire de Théodore de Mopsueste sur les Psaumes,* Studi e Testi 93, Vatican: Biblioteca Apostolica Vaticana, 1939. My English translation is forthcoming.

[7] *Commentarii in Psalmos I-L,* CCG 6, Turnhout: Brepols, 1980. My English translation is forthcoming

[8] The evidence in Chrysostom's case I have presented in my translation, 4-5. Facundus of Hermianae, *Pro defensione trium capitulorum* 3,6 (PL 67.602) says as much for Theodore.

[9] Cf my translation, *Theodoret of Cyrus. Commentary on the Psalms.*

[10] Chrysostom (who has left us no preface to his large collection) raises no quibble about Davidic authorship of the Psalms, nor does he raise any question about the psalm titles, as did Diodore.

[11] *Bibliotheca* 172-74 (PG 103.504).

[12] The text of these four appear in PG 55.155-167,499-528, there being no modern critical edition.

[13] The evidence for the ἑρμηνεῖαι being delivered as homilies in Antioch I have assembled in my article, "Chrysostom's *Commentary on the Psalms*: homilies or tracts?" 301-17.

[14] Cf Hom.10 on Genesis (PG 53.90), Hom. 29 on Genesis (PG 53.262). For an English translation of these homilies see my *St. John Chrysostom. Homilies on Genesis*, FOTC 74,82,87, Washington DC: Catholic University of America Press, 1986-92.

[15] Homily on Ps 42.

[16] Following Montfaucon, we may take as a clue his beginning the homily on Ps 42 by referring to his treatment of Melchizedek "the other day," this being found in the seventh of his eight Homilies against the Jews (cf PG 48.923-25), and so dated in late 387.

[17] W. Mayer has studied the nature and distribution of Chrysostom's congregations in churches in Antioch and Constantinople in "John Chrysostom: extraordinary preacher, ordinary audience" in M. B. Cunningham, P. Allen (edd.), *Preacher and Audience*, Leiden: Brill, 1998, 105-37.

[18] Montfaucon, PG 55.155-56, details the practice as Athanasius knew it. For the practice in Chrysostom's large collection of Psalm homilies, see the introduction to my translation, 11.

[19] Cf my "The spirituality of Chrysostom's *Commentary on the Psalms*," *Journal of Early Christian Studies* 5 (1997) 569-79.

[20] *The Spirituality of the New Testament and the Fathers*, Eng. trans., London: Burns & Oates, 1963, 444.

[21] Cf Mayer, "Extraordinary preacher," 123: "It is clear that at Constantinople a number of women who were once regularly in attendance have recently taken offense at Chrysostom and transferred their loyalties elsewhere."

[22] Second homily on Ps 49.16.

[23] First homily on Ps 49.16.

[24] Cf the warning by J. N. D. Kelly, *Golden Mouth. The Story of John Chrysostom, Ascetic, Preacher, Bishop*, Ithaca NY: Cornell University Press, 1995, 94: "Neither John, nor any Christian teacher for centuries to come, was properly equipped to carry out exegesis as we have come to understand it. He could not be expected to understand the nature of Old Testament writings" – the latter limitation being debatable.

[25] Jerome speaks of the three forms of the LXX current in his time in his *Praef. In Paral.* (PL 28.1324-25), and describes it as "popular" and "Lucianic" in *Ep.* 106.2 (PL 22.838), that is, a revision by the scholar-priest of Antioch a century earlier.

[26] I have done this in the introduction to the translations of Chrysostom's and Theodoret's Psalm Commentaries.

[27] Cf my "Chrysostom, interpreter of the Psalms," *Estudios Bíblicos* 56 (1998) 61-74.

²⁸ Cf my "Psalm 45: a *locus classicus* for patristic thinking on biblical inspiration," *Studia Patristica* 25 (1993) 95-100.

²⁹ Cf my articles, "On looking again at *synkatabasis*," *Prudentia* 13 (1981) 3-11; "*Akribeia*: a principle of Chrysostom's exegesis," *Colloquium* 15 (Oct. 1981) 32-36.

³⁰ In the ninth century Photius excused him for some superficiality in commenting on the Psalms on the grounds of his pastoral purpose: "Now, it is not surprising if his attention to some of the expressions or interpretation or depth of insight was careless; after all, he never at any stage neglected what the ability of the listeners dictated and had relevance to their benefit and welfare" (*Bibliotheca* 174; PG 103.505).

³¹ Cf J. De Ghellinck, *Patrisque et moyen âge. Etudes d'histoire littéraire et doctrinal*, II *Introductions et compléments à l'étude de la patristique*, Paris: Desclée de de Brouwer, 1947.

Notes to Homily on Psalm 42

¹ Text edited by Bernard de Montfaucon, found in PG 55.155-67. Unlike the psalms Chrysostom commented on in his collection of fifty-eight homilies, in this case he is only using the opening verse (or two) of the psalm, sung as a response, as the basis of exhortation on a moral theme.

² Chrysostom treated of Melchizedek in the seventh of his Homilies against the Jews in late 387 in Antioch. He knows how to cajole his listeners with opening compliments.

³ Perhaps it was the attendance of some Christians at the Jewish festivals that provoked this venom and those homilies, the Jews being a force to be reckoned with in Antioch.

⁴ The Introduction deals with this practice of singing a responsorial verse or refrain, ὑπακοή.

⁵ We have seen Chrysostom to be an acute observer of human nature; he has no difficulty assembling a range of examples from daily life to support his theme, "Music hath charms."

⁶ Cf Eph 5.18-19. Chrysostom, like Theodoret after him, is concerned that people do not understand the psalms they sing in the liturgy, both commentators adopting a cognitive approach. The accent on "understanding" (found also in Diodore) may also be an implicit reflection of its mention in the title (omitted by him) as the LXX's inadequate rendering of Heb. *maskil*, probably a type of psalm.

⁷ Chrysostom implies his congregation is a male one.

⁸ Acts 16.25.

⁹ Ps 92.4. The homilist has parted company with his text somewhat to develop other concerns.

¹⁰ Elsewhere in his homilies Chrysostom can be cited for his acquaintance with the excesses of public entertainment of his time, as also for his idea of the domestic church, where a family prays, sings and reads the Bible together. Such a family ritual he classes as λειτουργία, λατρεία.

¹¹ With his accent on his congregation's understanding what they sing,

the phrase "for the time being" is a limited concession. Also, for Antiochene spirituality, the capital sin is indifference, ῥαθυμία, and the cardinal virtue enthusiasm, προθυμία.

[12] Cf Gal 5.17-18.

[13] Is it instances like Exod 14.15 that Chrysostom has in mind?

[14] Rom 8.26-27. As mentioned above, the homilist has the men in his congregation in focus, not denying this practice to women as well.

[15] 2 Cor 6.11. Finally the homilist returns to the text of the psalm.

[16] Ps 63.1, the identity of the translator unknown (there being no extant copy of the Hexapla to consult, which Chrysostom is presumably consulting), and the need to mention the fact likewise puzzling. In the collection of fifty-eight homilies on the Psalms, Chrysostom frequently cites – also anonymously – the ancient alternative versions associated with the names Aquila, Symmachus and Theodotion.

[17] Heb 11.27. Not concerned to move on through the psalm, Chrysostom goes off an another moral tangent.

[18] Cf Matt 19.21.

[19] Cf Matt 25.35-36.

[20] Isa 6.2-3, verses on which Chrysostom composed a special series of homilies. The warning against an anthropomorphic understanding of the divinity is predictable.

[21] Ps 45.3.

[22] Cf Exod 33.13.

[23] John 14.8. This eastern commentator both acknowledges the transcendent beauty of the divinity and our inability to approach it.

[24] 2 Cor 9.15; 1 Cor 2.9 (cf Isa 64.4); Rom 11.33. At some distance from his text, Chrysostom characteristically documents his argument liberally from the Scriptures, and Paul in particular.

[25] John 3.16.

[26] Isa 49.15.

[27] Matt 23.37; Ps 102.13,11.

[28] 2 Cor 5.20.

[29] Eph 1.20-21, the term "first-fruits" in reference to Jesus coming from 1 Cor 15.20.

[30] Pss 106.2; 116.12.

[31] We recognize in this style of homiletics the practice of preachers the world over choosing to appeal to baser motives.

[32] Ps 130.2. The theme of God's longsuffering mentioned in the heading to the commentary has not received much attention.

[33] Theodoret, too, a confirmed naturalist, and Theodore before him will at this point also mention the reputed habit of the deer (an idea stemming from Origen), Diodore mentioning only the deer's thirst.

[34] This is a frequent qualification in Chrysostom's mouth, evincing his belief in the divine inspiration of the biblical authors.

[35] An interesting detailing of the composition of the Christian community at worship. Presumably only an exclusively male congregation

needed to be on the alert against the temptress that this homilist often imagines as a threat to them.

³⁶ Cf 2 Cor 11.21-27; Rom 5.2-3; Col 1.24; Phil 1.29.

³⁷ Though the Antiochene text incorporates the additional epithet "strong," Chrysostom seems to know a version without it as well. Dahood tells us the one Heb. term is susceptible of both readings. As he finally moves beyond the responsorial verse, Chrysostom also interchanges the terms for love, ἀγάπη, ἔρος, φίλτρον.

³⁸ Chrysostom can at times credit the psalmist with an eschatology not generally credited to Old Testament authors.

³⁹ One has only to compare Chrysostom's commentary on a psalm (in his pulpit) with Diodore's, Theodore's and Theodoret's (as their desk) to see the impact of the homilist's use of his considerable rhetorical skills that won him his sobriquet.

⁴⁰ An Antiochene commentator expects his congregation to apply to the text (even if orally recited, as in their case) the same precision, ἀκρίβεια, as he does.

⁴¹ The pastoral function of the refrain or responsorium, ὑπακοή, is thus clear: it acts as a mnemonic or mantra for the worshipers, who can recall the content of the homily by reciting it later, especially when the homilist has drilled them in it and commented on it.

⁴² Ps111.1. The LXX rendering ἀνήρ is not so much out of place in Chrysostom's male congregation. Theodoret, in commenting on a similar phrase in Ps 1.1, will assure any women readers that they are not excluded (though not proceeding in his Commentary to honor his own principle).

⁴³ Chrysostom has moved from explaining the function of the psalm refrains to develop a favorite theme of his, the respective positions of rich and poor.

⁴⁴ Like preachers the world over, Chrysostom regrets the length of the homily, which has not touched on the bulk of the psalm. Though he can be dismissive of scholars, here he has to encourage the more studious of his congregation, φιλοπονώτεροι, to make up for his shortcomings; no others would have the books to do so. The (male) congregation will teach the refrains to their families. The synaxis may have terminated at this point, just as the fifty-eight homilies in the collection of the Psalter were delivered in a non-eucharistic gathering in a classroom; see the introduction to my translation.

Notes to the First Homily on Psalm 49.16

¹ Text edited by B. de Montfaucon, appearing in PG 55.499-512; cf CPG 4414. Chrysostom had commented on the whole of Ps 49 in the large collection of homilies (probably delivered in Antioch), and had found it very much grist to his mill. Perhaps to take advantage of recent developments in Constantinople, he now returns to deliver two homilies on a favorite locus, in the process losing sight of his text at times.

² The homilist employs metaphors that are traditional as well as apposite to begin, as often, by winning over his congregation with compliments.

The appropriateness of references to "disturbance" emerges when implicit mention is made below of recent political developments; see note 8.

[3] Sir 25.9; Matt 5.6.

[4] Isa 40.6-7. In berating those absent (by addressing his words to those present – a common practice with preachers) Chrysostom lets his extreme pique at their absence run to highly rhetorical condemnation of involvement in this-worldly concerns, which can amount to an unbalanced spirituality. See my article, "The spirituality of Chrysostom's *Commentary on the Psalms*."

[5] Gen 1.26. As often, Chrysostom is taking his time in reaching his theme for the day.

[6] We may find this reading of the book of Job uncritical, focusing only on the Job of the prose framework, not the disgruntled and dissatisfied Job of the verse, whose author directly challenges the other's theology. Again we find "scorn for all human things" a rather impractical ideal for Chrysostom's lay congregation, even if he did take seriously (before discounting) their claims of family responsibilities.

[7] After establishing in general the urgency and value of attending his homilies (twice a week), Chrysostom finally reaches the particular text which will demonstrate that value on this occasion.

[8] This description of the unreliability and danger of riches Chrysostom used also in his homilies on Eutropius, the consul-eunuch whose fall from grace and appeal for sanctuary in the Great Church in Constantinople occurred in mid-399; the event, touched on also at the beginning of the next homily on this text, confirms editor Montfaucon's dating of our homily. The preacher has not allowed a timely example to pass without making a wider application.

[9] Chrysostom further exploits the recent fall of Eutropius to draw a lesson for his congregation and for himself. He proceeds to recommend they use the verse like a motto or refrain, ὑπόθεσις (somewhat as in the case of the opening verse of Ps 42).

[10] As with modern preachers – at least where congregations do not have eyes glued to a book – in Chrysostom's practice the text was proclaimed and then preached upon.

[11] Job 29.15-16; 31.32. Chrysostom tries to salvage his name for balance in respect of material goods. He has, however, no solution for poverty in his society except to recommend handouts.

[12] If this remark seems less than logical, manuscripts differ in the readings they offer.

[13] The exchange between the preacher and his critics is somewhat clearer in the Greek, where formal differences in the pronouns are more easily recognizable. He acknowledges that he has a track record of championing the poor and criticizing the rich – as his earlier homily on this psalm (probably from his Antioch period) and the next homily on this text betray – and that he is incurring some unpopularity for it.

[14] At this point editor Montfaucon comments, "He says he is a shepherd

because at that time he was archbishop of Constantinople," to confirm the dating of the homily.

¹³ 2 Cor 2.9; cf Isa 64.4.

¹⁴ Matt 5.43; Luke 23.34, the local (Koine) NT text being one that included this verse.

¹⁵ Again we get the impression that men alone were present in the congregation, or alone in focus. In listing these groups of people we also gain the impression of someone with a shrewd grasp of social mores.

¹⁶ The metaphor of the pastor as surgeon is not original, but the preacher sustains it to good effect.

¹⁷ Gen 18.1-5. Chrysostom now develops his commentary on the psalm verse in the direction of hospitality, a logical enough development in recommending the rich not to neglect others – though in the collection of homilies he had moved rather to excoriate the rich for indulging in funerary excesses, the later psalm verses moving in that direction.

¹⁸ Cf Gen 14.14.

¹⁹ Matt 5.20.

²⁰ Cf Gen 15.5.

²¹ Gen 18.6.

²² Now that Gen 18 and not Ps 49 has become the text for commentary, Sarah – and with her women in general – comes into focus. The reference to a shared classroom, διδασκαλεῖον (the longer series of homilies was delivered in such a setting), which in some mss appears as δικαστήριον, courtroom, need not be taken to imply that women were present on this occasion.

²³ Cf Gen 2.18. The commentary now takes a new turn, on women's role and style of living – a theme on which Chrysostom elsewhere also waxed eloquent. Was any woman in Constantinople (e.g., the empress) particularly in focus?

²⁴ Cf 1 Tim 2.9. Chrysostom seems to envisage the Pauline text being recited "below" in the body of the church, and the women located "above" in galleries in churches so constructed when they did attend. Perhaps this suggests the Great Church as the venue for the homily (the length further suggesting it is not a eucharistic liturgy), as is true of the next homily.

²⁵ Eccl 8.1.

²⁶ Luke 16.24. Like all preachers, Chrysostom with studied rhetoric can paint a frightening picture of the last things.

²⁷ Gen 18.10.

²⁸ Cf Gen 24.3-4.

²⁹ We have noted above Chrysostom's shrewd observation of social habits – though in this case he seems to be digressing even from his digression, and will move on further to treat of women's indiscretion.

³⁰ The preacher has to keep repeating the verse to recall his (doubtless wilting) congregation to the original point of departure of the homily. It is certainly high time to move on to the second half of the verse.

³¹ These are exactly the excesses of rich people's lifestyle Chrysostom

satirizes in his homily on Ps 49 in the larger collection.

[32] The closing verses of Ps 49, not cited here, move on to this consideration of the futility of riches in the light of death and oblivion, and in the larger collection Chrysostom warmed to the theme, as he does here.

[33] The earlier homily on Ps 49, apparently delivered in Antioch, did not draw this comparison with martyrs' tombs. Perhaps Chrysostom's ministry in Constantinople (the emperor's residence), or the proximity to them of the Great Church in which he is perhaps preaching, makes such a comparison compelling.

[34] Predictably, after such a long homily of a rather rambling nature the preacher closes briskly with little peroration. The verb used does not necessarily imply that singing the verse is recommended.

Notes to the Second Homily on Psalm 49.16

[1] Text of the homily edited by B. de Montfaucon, appearing in PG 55; 511-18; cf CPG 4415. This rubric to the text of the homily acknowledges the practice of the bishop speaking after another cleric, as exemplified also in Chrysostom's homily on Isaiah 45.6-7. He begins by complimenting the first speaker, whose words account for the relative brevity of this second homily on the same psalm text. The question of poor attendance is not raised by Chrysostom.

[2] Cf Col 3.16.

[3] The previous homily on this text also touched briefly on recent sensational developments in Constantinople that seem to have involved the fall of the consul-eunuch Eutropius, which occurred in mid-399 –"just the other day," πρώην, he goes on to say. The metaphor of a storm at sea, if not original, is clearly appropriate.

[4] Chrysostom is referring to the practice in the church of the reading aloud, ἀνάγνωσις, of the scriptural text (set down in a lectionary, or selected in view of recent developments?) before the homilist's commentary on it, the imagery again quite hackneyed and proceeding to be very disparate.

[5] Like many a preacher, Chrysostom is sensitive on the question of regular participation by his congregation in the assemblies, συνάξεις, at which he preaches. This comment may account for the mention in the homily title of small numbers attending.

[6] This less hackneyed comparison Chrysostom had used in the previous homily, where we also had to question the helpfulness of these remarks for his lay congregation.

[7] In Chrysostom's mind, these are the signs of opulence, as rehearsed in his Antioch homily and in the homily previous to this. Can the audience of "the other day" be the same as this?

[8] In a society where Christian life was susceptible of varieties of belief and practice, it was necessary to qualify the ideal of faith as ὀρθή and zeal as "according to God."

[9] After repeating some of the content of the earlier homily, Chrysostom

now proceeds to break new ground in satirizing the hauteur of rich people intolerant of mixing with their fellows.

[10] If Chrysostom laments irregular attendance, he has only himself to blame when he so rabidly belabors the affluent members of his congregation.

[11] If the comparison strikes us as novel, we should note (as Montfaucon does) that Chrysostom used it also in another homily at this time, on the fall of Eutropius.

[12] The psalm text has been left well behind as Chrysostom dwells on the theme of misdirected wealth, prepared like many a preacher to turn the heat up.

[13] This was in fact the sentiment of the psalm verse, to which the preacher should return before concluding. Chrysostom relishes the notion of the rich man's vain hope for posthumous fame, the theme of the psalm's closing verses. He implies that this congregation has not heard it in his previous homily.

[14] Though we observed above that Chrysostom takes a moral and not an economic approach to poverty, failing to offer a solution to institutional poverty in his society, today's ecologists would resonate with his accent on the need for sustainable (and just) use of resources.

[15] 1 Cor 2.9; cf Isa 64.4. Chrysostom, preaching in his church at a synaxis that is probably eucharistic, lists the spiritual goods of all Christians in interesting fashion, stressing the sacraments – eucharist, baptism (including the "cleansing of sins," or is this a separate ritual?) – while not including the Church, let alone a sacrament peculiar to the clergy.

[16] Acts 10.4, the angel's encomium of Cornelius. The homily concludes with the customary peroration and doxology, not having gone to great length, as would be appropriate if the synaxis were eucharistic, and having touched on material only partly covered earlier.

Notes to Homily on Psalm 146.1

[1] Text of the homily edited by B. de Montfaucon, appearing in PG 55.519-28; cf CPG 4416. The capital sin, the reason for the Fall, is indifference, and hence the cardinal virtue is enthusiasm. Fasting is terminated before the commencement of Easter Sunday, Saturday (in Antioch, where it seems the homily is being delivered) evidently being available for a homily before Easter is celebrated.

[2] Again the imagery is appropriate, if not original.

[3] This final phrase differs in the mss. The text speaks of Holy Week as "the Great Week."

[4] The phrasing is indebted to a range of New Testament loci, especially Matt 12.29; Eph 2.14-17; Gal 3.13.

[5] Cf John 12.9.

[6] We learn from the homilies something of the civic customs of the time, and the relation of Church and State. There are limits to civic authority, Chrysostom briefly adds – perhaps prompted by v.3 of the psalm (on which

he had commented in the larger collection), "Do not put your trust in rulers."

⁷ Cf Luke 21.2. Is Chrysostom simply being self-effacing in referring to the widow's mites in the course of describing the Palm Sunday procession in his church?

⁸ Cf John 12.12-13 (who alone mentions palms specifically); Matt 21.8-9.

⁹ So, as in comment on Ps 42.1-2 above, Chrysostom is dealing with these verses from Ps 146 as a refrain, ὑπακοή, sung by the congregation as prescribed for Holy Saturday.

¹⁰ Chrysostom frequently reminds his congregations of the divine inspiration of the biblical authors (something he does not do at this point in his full commentary on Ps 146), and this leads on to citation of Ps 45, which for him and so many of the Fathers is a classic text for discussion of that charism. See my article, "Psalm 45: a *locus classicus* for patristic thinking on biblical inspiration." Theodoret, perhaps prompted by this comment, likewise mentions the Spirit's inspiration in comment on Ps 146.1.

¹¹ This is, of course, one aspect of inspired discourse, προφητεία, the unfettered flow of grace. But Antioch typically will also insist on the human author's contribution, Chrysostom in particular comparing an inspired author, προφήτης, to a shipwright working at his trade.

¹² Luke 16.24-29 loosely cited.

¹³ Chrysostom can be quoted for an even more elevating theology of the Scriptures, as the Word enfleshed in (another) incarnation. This notion of the biblical text as the still-eloquent image of the inspired authors is reflected in the respect shown it in eastern liturgies in particular.

¹⁴ Matt 22.42-44 quoting Ps 110.1, a text on which Chrysostom discoursed at length in his full commentary on that psalm, though not presenting this notion of the Scriptures as images of the authors.

¹⁵ This notion of the harmonious participation in worship of all right-minded believers Chrysostom developed also in commentary on Ps 42.1-2.

¹⁶ Cf Ps 150.6, which in fact does not proceed to make a particular address to the soul that Chrysostom exploits for his purposes.

¹⁷ Ps 63.1 LXX.

¹⁸ Ps 103.1. An Antiochene could not allow any dualism in creation.

¹⁹ Ps 19.1.

²⁰ Ps 104.24. Chrysostom clearly has a wide familiarity with the psalms, though strangely Pss 103 and 104 do not appear in his large collection.

²¹ 1 Cor 14.15.

²² 1 Thess 5.17-18.

²³ Cf Dan 3.25.

²⁴ Cf Acts 16.24-29.

²⁵ Matt 18.18. The account of Paul's liberation from the prison in Philippi, purportedly to illustrate the efficacy of hymn-singing, now takes over the homily, the psalm text left behind. Is it that the latter has been exhausted, and Chrysostom – to whom Paul is as dear as the psalmist – elaborates on the gripping story for its own sake?

[26] Acts 16.28.

[27] Acts 16.30.

[28] Matt 5.16.

[29] The text says simply that the jailer and his family were baptized. Chrysostom (hymn-singing now left far behind) uses the terminology of initiation, the verb μυσταγωγεῖν, reference to the washing of baptism and the eucharistic banquet, and proceeds to show Paul serving the jailer a meal, at which point Montfaucon observes, "It was not Paul who provided a meal for the jailer, but the jailer for Paul" (Acts 16.34).

[30] Cf Mark 2.3-12.

[31] After a brief acknowledgement that the day's theme was initially hymn-singing, Chrysostom then addresses a different topic, fasting and prayer, citing 1 Cor 7.5; Matt 17.21 (found in some mss including the Antiochene); Acts 13.3.

[32] On prayer, of course, Chrysostom has spoken to his congregations on many occasions; for example, in comment on Pss 4 & 7 in the large collection he lectures on "the art of prayer" – though typically for an Antiochene he never ascends to a mystical level, adopting as here a more pragmatic tack. See my article, "The spirituality of Chrystomstom's *Commentary on the Psalms*."

[33] 2 Cor 12.8-9.

[34] Ps 119.62.

[35] What prayers were prescribed for daily recitation is unclear. Montfaucon suggests that the mention of monks in nearby mountains, frequently referred to by Chrysostom in his Antioch days, possibly implies that the homily comes from his ministry there.

[36] For the Antiochenes the corollary of understanding the meaning of prayers (the psalms, e.g.) is concentration on this meaning. An intimate relationship in prayer can go without mention.

[37] Indifference, sloth, negligence, ῥᾳθυμία, we noted above, is for the Antiochenes (with their pragmatic approach to the spiritual life) the capital sin.

[38] The downside to this pedestrian approach to prayer, with the accent on cognition and rapt attention to formulas, is the danger of scruples, one would think.

[39] The homily closes on the theme of the value of prayer, no further reference being made to the psalm verse that highlighted rather the importance of singing or the significance of Holy Saturday.

General Index

Abraham, 39, 67, 95-102
ἀκρίβεια, 66, 140, 142
Alexandria, 56
Allen, P., 129, 130, 139
anthropomorphism, 66, 141
Antioch, *passim*
apophatic, 132
Aquila, 56
Aristeas, 7
Athanasius, 139
Aubineau, M., 138
Augustine, 6, 53, 54, 134
authorship, 66

baptism, 137, 146, 148
Barthélemy, D., 129
Baur, C., 129
Baruch, 18, 19
bishop, 36, 56, 57, 66, 136, 144, 145
Bouyer, L., 129
byzantine, 138

church, 22, 36, 46, 51, 54, 55, 60, 62, 72, 89, 105, 117, 135, 137, 140
communicatio idiomatum, 131
conservation, 63, 146
Constantinople, 54, 55, 56, 57, 61, 62, 105, 139, 142, 144, 145
creation, 147

creed, 1
Cunningham, M. B., 139

David, *passim*
deacon, 57
Deuteronomist, 137
Devreesse, R., 138
διδασκαλεῖον, 66, 144
Diodore of Tarsus, 54, 66, 138, 140, 141, 142
dogmatic, 137
Drewery, B., 129
dualism, 61, 136, 147

emperor, 105, 115
eucharist, 54, 56, 57, 113, 142, 144, 146, 148
exegesis, 1, 54, 64, 139
ἐξομολόγησις, 137
Eutropius, 56, 64, 67, 68, 143

Facundus of Hermianae, 138
faith, 145
Fall, 135, 146
fasting, 148
Fernández Marcos, N., 129
Fronto de Duc, 134

genre, 58
Ghellinck, J. de, 140
grace, 137

147

Index of Biblical Citations

Made in the USA
Middletown, DE
07 August 2023

36343539R00094